Reviews

"Her cooking is superb, very tasty, delicious, and healthy. Great food and lessons learned over the years as she educates the customers in her classes."

– Chris King-David, Bennett Realty Solutions Greenbelt, MD

"Very efficient teacher and presenter. Also, very competent cook and caterer."

– Inskip Allsop, Golden Rule Holistic, Wilmington, DE

"I have had the pleasure of eating from Dorrel's table over the past 40 + years and was very   happy when I bought her first cookbook *The Transitional Cookbook*. It has been a great help in getting my family to enjoy some of the Caribbean Meals with a vegan twist. I know that her new cookbook *Something Different* will also be an invaluable part of your cooking experience."

– Paulette Mascoe-Bennett, RN,

"I highly recommend this cookbook. You can taste the love in every bite of Ms. Dorrel's cooking. If you ever have the pleasure of being in her company listening to talk about her love for cooking and God will warm your heart."

– Danielle S. Lee, Owner of DSLee Travel, LLC. Founder of Brown Girls International

"I am excitedly looking forward to this new cookbook *Something Different*. Ms. Dorrel has a way of creating different tastes and textures with everyday ingredients. She is creative in that way. Her recipes encourage the cook to change their perspective about cooking the same recipes in the same ways."

– Laisha V. Wright, Security Coordinator Seventh-day Adventist World Headquarters

"I am truly excited for the release of this second cookbook, *Something Different*. It is a One Stop Shop for excellent healthy recipes, not just for inside but for outside of the body too! The Spiritizers add a special spiritual touch that sets this cookbook apart from the others."

– Samois R., mother of four, Senior Office Assistant, Department of In-House Operations Seventh-day Adventist World Headquarters Office

"Every year there are hundreds of cookbooks being published and you try to decide which one to choose, but *Something Different* is one of a kind. The author Dorrel McLaren has compiled these recipes with love and from experience with her culinary skills she focuses on individual's health and well-being.

"As a Clinician who believes and knows what you eat has an effect on your well-being, this cookbook gives you recipes that are wholesome and healthy. I would recommend this cookbook to anyone who is looking for something different in their daily cooking experience. I would give this cookbook a 5."

– Lilieth Occenad, FNP-C, Clinician Family Nurse Practitioner

"Congratulations on your new book *Something Different*. I like the title and having attended your workshop on bread making where you showed us how to make bread in a different way, I can endorse the current title of your new book. *Something Different* as I know you to do your cooking differently with a lot of creativity. You provide substitutes that most people are not aware of but need to know and that stops the question 'What Shall I use in a particular recipe, etc.'

– Joyce B. Nvairo, Lifestyle Integration Expert, Certified Health Coach, Protocol and Etiquette Consultant, Past President PEAN SDA Toastmasters Club, Amazing Balance International Group, LLC

"This beautifully written gorgeously illustrated cookbook is a definitive text for anyone wanting to learn how to cook delicious easy plant-base meals to enhance their overall health. Dorrel, an impressive self-taught Jamaican vegan chef, is committed to teaching family/friends/colleagues and anyone in her hearing that wonderful heart and kidney health benefits of a plant-base diet. I have been a frontline benefactor of her mouthwatering vegan meals and I can say with surety that going plant-base significantly helped to reduce my high blood pressure over 20 years ago. When I say following the plant-base recipes in this cookbook will change your life for the better."

– Lieutenant Colonel Verona Boucher, USAF, Retired

"Mrs. Dorrel McLaren is an amazing cook. The recipes in her cookbook have been tried and proven to be beneficial for my family, my friends, and me. I have personally tasted some of the menus from her kitchen and that are also in her cookbook. I was very satisfied, and I am thankful that I have her amazing cookbook in my possession. Keep on writing these books to help those of us who need help in planning menus for our families. Thank you."

– Dr. Paulette Terrelonge, New York School System

"As one who is personally acquainted with Dorrel McLaren, I have had the pleasure of enjoying the delectable cuisines she produces in her kitchen over many years. It is my pleasure to endorse her new cookbook *Something Different*. I have found Dorrel's main dishes to be original finger liking mouthwatering and with a flare of professionalism in her presentation. At church functions, parties, banquets, or any other venues, her dishes are always sought out and quickly disappear. Her background in food, nutrition and hospitality predisposes her to an above average knowledge in a plant base diet. Without question, this new cookbook is a must-have for every kitchen."

– Leanora Salmon, R.N., Washington Adventist Hospital

Eden's Hope Ministries Presents

Something Different
A Healthy Taste of the Caribbean

*Dorrel R. McLaren
with Pharmacist
Earl A. McLaren*

TEACH Services, Inc.
PUBLISHING
www.TEACHServices.com • (800) 367-1844

World rights reserved. This book or any portion thereof may not be copied or reproduced in any form or manner whatever, except as provided by law, without the written permission of the publisher, except by a reviewer who may quote brief passages in a review.

The author assumes full responsibility for the accuracy of all facts and quotations as cited in this book. The opinions expressed in this book are the author's personal views and interpretations, and do not necessarily reflect those of the publisher.

This book is provided with the understanding that the publisher is not engaged in giving spiritual, legal, medical, or other professional advice. If authoritative advice is needed, the reader should seek the counsel of a competent professional.

Copyright © 2023 Dorrel R. McLaren

Copyright © 2023 TEACH Services, Inc.

ISBN-13: 978-1-4796-1506-3 (Paperback)

ISBN-13: 978-1-4796-1507-0 (ePub)

Library of Congress Control Number: 2023902849

Bible texts marked (KJV) are taken from the King James Version of the Bible. Public domain.

Bible texts marked (AKJV) are taken from the Authorized King James Version of the Bible, reproduced by permission of Cambridge University Press, the Crown's patentee in the UK.

Bible texts marked (NKJV) are taken from the New King James Version®. Copyright © 1982 by Thomas Nelson. Used by permission. All rights reserved.

Bible texts marked (NIV) are taken from the Holy Bible, New International Version®, NIV® Copyright © 1973, 1978, 1984, 2011 by Biblica, Inc.® Used by permission. All rights reserved worldwide.

Bible texts marked (NLT) are taken from the Holy Bible, New Living Translation, Copyright © 1996, 2004, 2015 by Tyndale House Foundation. Used by permission of Tyndale House publishers, Inc., Carol Stream, Illinois, 60188. All rights reserved.

Bible texts marked (NASB 1995) are taken from the New American Standard Bible®, Copyright © 1960, 1971, 1977, 1995 by The Lockman Foundation. All rights reserved.

Bible texts marked (ESV) are taken from The Holy Bible, English Standard Version. ESV® Text Edition: 2016. Copyright © 2001 by Crossway Bibles, a publishing ministry of Good News Publishers.

If you would like to contact the author regarding speaking engagements, health seminars and cooking classes, visit: https://edenshopeministries.com/

Table of Contents

Foreword 9

Dedication 11

Acknowledgements 13

Introduction 15

Chapter 1—Breakfast, Smoothies, Beverages, and More 17

Chapter 2—Soups and Stews 60

Chapter 3—Vegetables, Salads, and Dressings 75

Chapter 4—Entrées 89

Chapter 5—Rice, Casseroles, and Sauces 112

Chapter 6—Sandwiches, Spreads, and Pestos 127

Chapter 7—Deserts, Breads, and Rolls 149

Chapter 8—Seasonings and Spices 162

Chapter 9—Miscellaneous 167

Chapter 10—Tasty This and That 176

Chapter 11—Helpful Tips and More 184

Chapter 12—Pantry and Freezer 190

Chapter 13 —Still Something More 193

Resources 201

References 201

Index 202

About the Authors 212

Foreword

Health is our greatest treasure and we would do well to seek out how best we might preserve it. After all, let us not be like those who spend their health in order to gain wealth, only to have to spend their wealth seeking to regain their health. But as we all know, a balanced, nutritious diet is essential for maintaining good health. In fact, a lot of the ill-health afflicting the world today stems from poor food choices. Most of us don't eat to maximize our health and well-being. One of the big reasons for that is the perception that healthy food is either expensive, difficult to prepare, or doesn't taste good. Well, Dorrel McLaren, Certified Vegetarian Food Instructor, has come along to put that misperception to rest with this unique cookbook called *Something Different*.

What makes this cookbook distinctive is the overall approach to healthy cooking that she incorporates in her recipes. Her emphasis—which is very evident in this volume—has always been: 1) easy-to-make recipes that are healthy and great-tasting; 2) recipes made with readily available ingredients; and 3) dishes that are quick and easy to prepare. After all, who wants to slave away in the kitchen in order to prepare a tasty, healthy meal? You will love her unique, tempting recipes that incorporate the principles of vegetarianism, which is enjoying a resurgence among the health conscious, and has found strong support from many well-known, nutritionally conscious doctors, such as Dr. Neil Barnard and Caldwell Esselstyn.

Another important feature of this book is its inclusion of devotional readings. These pieces, written by her husband, Dr. Earl McLaren, are meant to address our spiritual health. It is a well-known fact that health involves more than just our physical wellbeing—it also includes our mind, emotions, and spirit. It is not enough to feed our bodies if we neglect to feed our souls. Someone once said it's better to eat pie with friends than broccoli alone. And guess what? That is truly so. To be lonely, depressed, and sad can do as much damage—maybe even more so—than a poor food choice. So, as you peruse this volume, you will find great spiritual gems to encourage, motivate, and inspire. You will also find other great health tidbits, all designed to equip you to live the best life you can. Expect to spend many exciting, mouthwatering moments in your kitchen as you try one, then another, and still another, of Dorrel's innovative, exciting, nutritious, and totally tasty recipes. Here's to great eating and better living!

—Inskip Allsop, ND, CNC

Dedication

This book is dedicated to my husband, Earl; my son, Derrol; my daughter, Samois; and all the other family members and friends who have eaten the hundreds of meals from test recipes over many years.

Many have changed or modified their eating habits as a result and have testified that their lives have been better doing so. To that we say … "To God be the glory, great things He has done!"

Acknowledgements

Our deepest gratitude to our Supreme Provider, God, for making available to us the abundance of fruits, vegetables, grains, legumes, nuts, seeds, and herbs in their varied colors, tastes, shapes, sizes, and nutrients. With everlasting love, He has provided for our nutritional needs, so we may eat freely and be fit to go on His errands, to help prepare souls for His kingdom. Father, we love you. Help us to always eat just enough to be nourished for the journey.

Introduction

Thank you for making an important decision to purchase this *Something Different Cookbook*!

My earliest memories of cooking were with "Granny," my dear sweet grandmother who always tried to teach me the value of quality as opposed to quantity. As I grew older and started my family, and understood the value of good nutrition, I realized that she was a gourmet cook without knowing what that meant in those times.

In the course of time, and with access to more health information, I have learned that the kitchen plays a great role in nutrition and good health, and that what we eat will: either speed up, slow down, or even arrest or prevent processes in our bodies. It is never too late to begin eating for optimal nourishment, and as we age, it becomes even more important to do so. This realization has both inspired and created the passion in me to teach and demonstrate how to prepare tasty, nutritious foods without spending all day in the kitchen.

The body has the built-in tendency to mend itself if it is given the proper nutrients, so the sooner we begin to give it the right foods, the sooner it will begin to reverse any—or at least some—of the damage that has already been done.

Some of the foods we eat will heal us, while others may do us harm, but it is important to remember that there are ways to prepare healthy meals with healing foods. Great nutritious meals prepared in your kitchen laboratory will keep you out of the doctor's laboratory! This cookbook seeks to help in the process of doing just that—to help you to prepare tasty meals, eat well, and enjoy the journey because every mouthful of what you eat matters to your present and future health.

Chapter 1

Breakfast, Smoothies, Beverages, and More...

Spiritizer

Emergency and Disaster Preparedness

Devotional thought presented for the discussion topic on the Forum at GCE, "Emergency and Disaster Preparedness."

In Matthew chapter 24 the disciples brought Jesus' attention to the temple at Jerusalem. They had heard that Jesus told the rulers that their house would be left desolate. They wanted to know if Jesus was really talking about the temple with its magnificent architecture and its majestic beauty.

Jesus said, "Ah yes, beautiful, isn't it? Sad though, that the day is coming when not one of these stones will be left on another."

The disciples began to understand that Jesus was referring to end time events so when they retired on the mountainside they continued with their inquiry: "So please tell us more Jesus; when shall these things be—the signs of your coming and the end of the world?"

Jesus followed with a litany of signs and events that will be indicative of last day events and His return. This He did so that not just the disciples, but the people of God, would be prepared for the earth's final events and His eminent return.

Let's be prepared for any potential emergency and disaster—but more so, let's be prepared for the coming of our Lord and Savior, Jesus Christ.

The Bible is replete with stories, parables, and warnings that prompt the believer to be discerning, vigilant, and prepared for the times in which we live.

Yes. There is a biblical basis for preparedness.

The Laodicean church says: "I am rich, and increased with goods, and have need of nothing" (Rev. 3:17, KJV). But our spiritual diagnosis reveals poverty, wretchedness, nakedness, and blindness, and one of the treatments recommended is spiritual eye ointment so that we can discern the times in which we live. Sometimes we miss what is right in front of us. Don't forget, the priest held Jesus in his arms and gave him the customary blessing but never knew that he was holding the High Priest and his Savior.

Let's be prepared for any potential emergency and disaster—but more so, let's be prepared for the coming of our Lord and Savior, Jesus Christ.

Father, thank You for not leaving us clueless about end of time happenings. You have given us that shout out in clarion tones: "look up ... for your redemption draweth nigh" (Luke 21:28, AKJV). May Your Holy Spirit impart unto us discernment, awareness, training, skills and abilities that will prepare us for the times we live in, and for Your soon coming. Amen.

Breakfast, Smoothies, Beverages, and more... ◆ 19

Confetti Scramble

1 small onion, chopped
¼ cup each of red, green, and yellow peppers
2 cloves garlic, pressed
2 tablespoons coconut oil
2 tablespoons nutritional yeast
1 teaspoon black Indian salt
½ teaspoon turmeric
1 pound very firm tofu, drained

Method

Sauté onions, peppers and garlic with oil for three minutes. Add nutritional yeast, salt, and turmeric to tofu and mash with a fork and add to pot. Blend well and continue to sauté for another ten minutes.

Mock Omelet

1 pound medium-firm tofu, drained
¼ cup raw cashews
½ cup flour
½ cup water
1 teaspoon black Indian salt
1–2 tablespoons nutritional yeast
¼ teaspoon turmeric
2 stalks scallion

Method

Grease iron skillet with coconut oil and heat on medium setting.

Place all ingredients into blender and whiz thoroughly. Pour into hot skillet and cover. Reduce heat to low. Allow to cook for 8–10 minutes.

Flip over by inverting into a plate. Slide off into skillet and cook for another 8–10 minutes on that side. Do not allow to burn.

Serving suggestion: Fill omelet with sautéed veggies such as spinach, onions, and mushrooms.

Patty's Granola

Mix together in a large bowl:
12 cups rolled oats (42 oz. container)
⅔ cup brown sugar
1 cup wheat germ
2 cups unsweetened coconut flakes
½ cup flax meal
3 cups mixed chopped nuts
1 cup chopped dates
1 cup raisins*

Mix together in a glass measuring cup:
¾ cup canola oil
¾ cup honey or agave
1 tablespoon vanilla extract

Method

Pour wet ingredients over dry ingredients and mix well. Spread onto a large cookie sheet. Bake for 1 hour and 20 minutes at 300 degrees. Stir every 20 minutes.

*Remove from oven and add raisins.

Mix well and store in airtight containers or bags when cool.

Amazing Gluten-Free Granola

Mix together in a large bowl:
1 cup raw pumpkin seeds
1 cup pecan pieces
1 cup raw almonds
1 cup chopped dates
½ cup hemp seeds
1 tablespoon chia seeds
½ cup uncooked quinoa
2 tablespoons flax seeds
¼ teaspoon salt

Mix together in a glass measuring cup or small bowl:
3 tablespoons coconut oil
3–4 packets stevia (optional)
4 tablespoons maple syrup
1 tablespoon vanilla

*1 cup unsweetened coconut flakes
*1 cup cranberries

Method

Pour wet ingredients over dry ingredients and mix well. Bake at 325 degrees for 25 minutes, stirring occasionally.
*Remove from oven and add coconut flakes and cranberries. Return to oven for an additional 5–8 minutes. Do not allow coconut flakes to burn. Store in airtight container when thoroughly cooled.

Simple Granola

Mix together in a large bowl:
12 cups old-fashioned rolled oats
1 cup multigrain or whole wheat flour
1½ cups unsweetened coconut flakes
1½ cups pecan pieces

Mix together in a glass measuring cup:
1½ cups pineapple juice
1 cup brown sugar
½ cup canola oil
1 tablespoon vanilla extract
1 teaspoon sea salt

Method

Pour wet ingredients over dry ingredients and mix well. Spread on a cookie sheet and bake at 300 degrees for about 2 hours. Stir often. Do not allow to burn. Store in airtight container when thoroughly cooled.

Cashew Cream for Granola

2 cups raw cashews, soaked over night
½ cup maple syrup (more if you desire more sweetener)
⅛ teaspoon sea salt
½ cup almond milk (more or less depending on how thick or thin you want cream)
1 teaspoon vanilla extract

Method

Blend ingredients in a strong blender until smooth and creamy.

Serving suggestion: You may add fresh berries and sliced bananas to granola into a glass container in layers, and pour cream over top to make a delicious parfait.

Applesauce Cream

1 cup apple sauce
1 cup raw cashews, soaked overnight
½ teaspoon cinnamon powder

Method

Blend all ingredients in a blender until creamy.

Banana Yogurt and Berries

1 ripe banana
10 oz. silken soft tofu
3–4 tablespoons fresh lemon juice
2–4 tablespoons maple syrup
Pinch of salt
2 cups strawberries

Method

Blend the banana, tofu, lemon juice, maple syrup, and salt until smooth and creamy. Pour over berries and enjoy.

Buckwheat Breakfast Burritos

¼ cup red onion, chopped
½ cup green pepper, chopped
½ cup red pepper, chopped
2 tablespoons unrefined coconut oil
2 vegetarian bouillon cubes
1 pound firm tofu, crumbled
¼ cup buckwheat groats, prepared (see recipe following)
2 tablespoons nutritional yeast
1 (15.5-ounce) can black beans, drained and rinsed
4–6 vegetarian sausages (links or patties), minced
Dash of red pepper flakes (optional)
Salt and pepper to taste (optional)
10 large whole wheat or corn tortillas

Method

Sauté onion and peppers with coconut oil for three minutes on medium fire. Dissolve bouillon cubes into sautéed ingredients and blend well. Add tofu, buckwheat groats, nutritional yeast, and stir occasionally until heated through. Add all other ingredients and keep stirring for additional 3–5 minutes.

Warm tortillas on a griddle for a few seconds to make it easy to fold. Spoon ¼ cup mixture onto each tortilla and fold like burrito.

You may also fry burrito lightly on both sides in coconut oil.

Breakfast, Smoothies, Beverages, and more... ◆ 25

Overnight Prepared Buckwheat Groats

¼ cup buckwheat groats, rinsed
1 cup water
Salt to taste

Method

Place ingredients in a small saucepan and bring to a roaring boil for 1 minute.

Turn heat off and place lid on pot. Leave overnight on stove top.

Groats will be ready for use in the morning.

Note: Excess cooked groats may be used as hot cereal. Just add milk and reheat on stove top. Add favorite toppings such as raisins and berries, or your favorite fruit, and sweeten if you desire.

Vegetable Quesadillas

4 large tortilla wraps (whole wheat, spinach, or plain)
½ cup shredded vegan cheese of choice
½ cup vegetarian deli meat slices of choice, chopped
¼ cup green pepper, chopped
¼ cup red pepper, chopped
1 cup fresh spinach leaves
Taco sauce (optional)

Method

Spray cooking spray or olive oil onto tortilla wrap and place sprayed side down on griddle or skillet. Warm over low to medium heat. Layer ingredients onto tortilla, then place another tortilla on top and spray.

Press quesadilla down with spatula until bottom of tortilla is slightly brown, then turn over and press down until layers are heated through and cheese is melted. Cut into quarters and enjoy with salsa, soup, or salad.

Serving suggestion: Best when eaten hot. You may add any filling you want into your quesadillas.

Potato Waffles

8 cups grated potatoes with skin on (about 6–8 medium potatoes)
4 tablespoons unrefined coconut oil
4 tablespoons yellow cornmeal
2–4 tablespoons spelt flour
4 tablespoons nutritional yeast
2 tablespoons vegetarian chicken-style seasoning of choice
⅓ cup yellow onions, chopped

Method

Combine all ingredients in a bowl and mix well. Add mixture ½ cup at a time into oiled and preheated greased waffle iron. Bake 7–10 minutes.

Hearty Waffles

1 cup whole wheat flour
1 cup spelt flour
½ cup soy flour
1 cup pecan and cashew mix
½ cup wheat germ
1 teaspoon baking powder
1 teaspoon baking soda
2½ cups soy milk (add more if batter is too thick, less if too thin)
½ cup honey or agave (optional)
1 teaspoon fresh grated nutmeg
1 teaspoon sea salt

Method

Grind pecan and cashew mix in a food processor. Combine all dry ingredients into a medium bowl, and wet ingredients into another bowl.

Pour dry ingredients into bowl with wet ingredients and mix thoroughly to make a batter.

Using a ⅓ measuring cup, pour batter onto greased hot waffle griddle and cook until golden brown. Serve with your favorite fruit and syrup.

Gram Frittata

½ cup garbanzo flour
1 pound firm tofu
1 teaspoon Indian black salt
½ teaspoon turmeric
1 tablespoon cornstarch
2 cloves garlic, minced
2 tablespoons onion, chopped
½ cup water

Method

Combine ingredients in a bowl and mix well. Let sit in bowl for 10 minutes on counter before placing mixture into a shallow baking dish. Bake for 25–30 minutes at 350 degrees.

Vegetable Bacon

2 tablespoons olive oil
½ cup soy sauce
½ teaspoon paprika
¼ cup maple syrup
1 teaspoon liquid smoke
1 eggplant, sliced in long slices

Method

Combine the olive oil, soy sauce, paprika, maple syrup, and liquid smoke in a bowl. Mix well. Brush each side of the eggplant slices. Place eggplant on greased cookie sheet and bake at 300 degrees for 30–45 minutes. Turn eggplant slices halfway through. Do not allow to burn. Feel free to substitute pressed, firm tofu slices or thinly sliced carrot for the eggplant.

Better Than Butter

1 cup water
1 tablespoon sea salt, slightly rounded
1¼ cups virgin coconut oil
¾ cup extra virgin olive oil
2 tablespoons liquid lecithin
3 tablespoons flaxseed oil

Method

Mix water and salt together and set aside. Place the coconut oil, olive oil, liquid lecithin, and flaxseed oil in a blender and blend until smooth. While blender is still running, slowly pour salted water into oil mix. Blend until mixture is creamy and smooth and looks like butter. Pour into containers and chill in refrigerator. If separation occurs due to warming, simply stir and re-chill. This will keep up to three weeks when kept in the fridge after use.

Easy Pancakes

¾ cup spelt flour or wheat flour
½ teaspoon baking soda
3 tablespoons brown sugar
1 cup almond milk
1 teaspoon vanilla
½ stick soy margarine, melted
1 cup fresh mixed berries, or 1 cup craisins
½ teaspoon sea salt

Method

Place all ingredients into a large glass measuring cup with spout and mix (do not over mix; it is not necessary to get rid of all the lumps). Pour onto a hot griddle in desired pancake size and cook on both sides until golden brown.

Fluffy Banana Pancakes

2 ripe bananas, mashed into a bowl
1¼ cup almond milk
3½ teaspoons baking powder
1 teaspoon salt
2 tablespoons melted vegan butter or the Better than Butter recipe found in this book (p. 28)
1½ cups flour of choice
1½ cups fresh or frozen blueberries

Method

In the order as written, place all ingredients into bowl with bananas and mix. Make pancakes on hot griddle and enjoy with maple syrup.

Apple Tortilla Delite

1 large apple, peeled and cored and cut into pieces
1–2 tablespoons brown sugar, honey, or maple syrup
Dash of cinnamon and nutmeg
Juice from ½ lime or lemon
1 teaspoon oil
Whole wheat tortillas

Method

Mix the apple pieces, brown sugar, cinnamon, nutmeg, lime or lemon juice, and oil together in a bowl. Sauté apple mixture over medium heat until apples are soft. Warm tortillas and fill with the sautéed apples.

Serving suggestion: You may also use sliced, ripe bananas or any fruit of choice. Sauté fruit ahead of time and refrigerate. Then, when ready to eat, wrap in soft tortilla and warm in toaster oven for a few minutes. For a treat, serve with a scoop of vegan ice-cream. This is also a great topping for pancakes.

Tofu Crème Fraîche

16 ounces vegan cream cheese
8 ounces Mori-Nu® soft tofu
2 tablespoons fresh lemon juice
¼ cup almond milk
½ teaspoon pink Himalayan salt

Method

Place all ingredients in a high-speed blender and blend until smooth and creamy. Refrigerate for at least one hour to set before use. May be added to hot cereals, fruit salads, and desserts for creaminess.

Almond Crème Fraîche

2 cups raw almond, soaked over night
3 tablespoons canola oil
2 tablespoons fresh lemon juice
½ cup water
1 teaspoon salt

Method

Place all ingredients in a high-speed blender and blend until smooth and creamy. Refrigerate for at least one hour to set before use.

This may be used to thicken soups and sauces. You may also add confectioner's sugar to add some creaminess with a touch of sweetness to fruit salad, pies, or other desserts.

Vegetarian Fritters

1 cup chopped vegetarian meat of choice
1½ cups flour
1¼ teaspoons baking powder
1 teaspoon fresh thyme leaves
2 stalks scallion, finely chopped
1 small onion, chopped
¼ teaspoon black pepper
Salt to taste
¾ cup water (approximately)
Oil for frying

Method

Combine all dry ingredients into a bowl and slowly add water to form a thick batter. Drop fritters with a large spoon into hot oil and fry both sides on medium-high until brown. Drain on wire rack.

Bean Fritters

2 cups dried black-eyed peas, soaked in water overnight
1 medium onion, finely chopped
Small piece of hot pepper, chopped (optional)
1½ cups water
Salt to taste
Oil for frying

Method

Rub soaked beans between hands to remove skin (keep skin and add into mixture before frying). Place skinned beans into a food processor or use a mortar and pestle to beat until smooth. Place into a bowl and add all other ingredients. Drop batter into hot oil and fry until brown on each side.

Note: Omit the water and use coconut milk, wrap mixture tightly in dasheen leaves, and steam for about 30–45 minutes, slice thin into steaks, and fry.

Oven Potatoes

2 pounds small potatoes, washed and cut in halves
4 cloves fresh garlic, crushed
1 tablespoon dried oregano
2 tablespoons nutritional yeast
1 tablespoon vegetarian chicken-style seasoning
1 teaspoon dried rosemary
3 tablespoons olive oil
Salt to taste

Method

Partially cook potatoes in salted water—about 7 minutes. Place all other ingredients in a 9x13-inch glass baking dish and mix well. Add the partially cooked potatoes to the glass dish and stir to allow seasonings to coat evenly. Cover loosely with aluminum foil and bake for 30–45 minutes at 350 degrees, stirring occasionally.

Spicy Sausage

Mix together in a large bowl:
2¼ cups vital wheat gluten flour
½ cup nutritional yeast
¼ cup garbanzo flour
2 tablespoons beef-style seasoning
2 teaspoons onion powder
2 teaspoons garlic powder
2 teaspoons smoked paprika
1 teaspoon dried chili flakes
1 teaspoon dried oregano
1–2 tablespoon fennel seeds
1 teaspoon marjoram
1 teaspoon sea salt
Fresh coarsely ground black pepper
Pinch of ground allspice

Mix in a small bowl or measuring cup:
2¼ cups water
8 cloves garlic, minced or pressed
2 tablespoons olive oil
2 tablespoon soy sauce

Method

Blend the dry ingredients in the large bowl well. Whisk together the water, garlic, olive oil, and soy sauce, and mix into dry ingredients. Stir with a spoon until well blended.

Scoop ½ cup of dough at a time and shape into logs.

Wrap with cheese cloth or aluminum foil and steam for 45 minutes. Slice and lightly fry on both sides. Keep in freezer until ready to use.

Serving suggestion: Enjoy as a breakfast or dinner entrée. You may sauté onions, peppers, and tomatoes in olive oil, and add tomato ketchup to create a sauce, then add sausage pieces and allow to absorb the flavor of the sauce.

Soppy's Trinidad Coconut Bake

2 cups white flour
4 cups whole wheat flour
½ cup wheat bran
4 tablespoons brown sugar

1½ teaspoons salt
2 tablespoons active dry yeast (instant is great)
3 cups grated coconut
½ cup extra virgin coconut oil (melted)
2–2½ cups water

Method

Mix the flours, wheat bran, brown sugar, salt, and active dry yeast together in a large bowl. (If using pre-grated coconut, add to dry ingredients.) Stir together in a separate bowl or measuring cup the coconut oil and water. Create a well in the middle of the flour and pour the liquid in slowly, mixing with a large spoon. Continue mixing until too stiff to continue to use spoon.

At this point begin kneading the mixture until it no longer sticks to hands. (If dough is still sticky, add a little extra flour and continue kneading.) Be sure to knead for about 10 minutes until dough is springy.

Cover dough and let rest for approximately 30 minutes. Divide into two balls. Place "balls" on two greased baking sheets and flatten out to approximately ½ inch thickness. (Trinidadians usually find 1½ inches to be sufficient thickness.)

Place into preheated oven at 350 degrees and bake for 15 to 20 minutes or until top is golden brown.

Tunol

1 medium sized onion, or 2 sprigs scallion, finely chopped
½ large sweet pepper, finely chopped
1 large firm tomato, finely chopped
1 clove garlic, crushed or grated
1 (12-ounce) roll of frozen vegetarian tuna (canned Tuno® may be substituted), thawed and mashed
⅛ teaspoon cayenne (reduce this quantity if very sensitive to pepper; increase if you like it hot)
Onion powder and garlic salt to taste
2–3 tablespoons coconut oil

Method

Sauté onion, sweet pepper, tomato, and garlic over medium heat without oil until onion is translucent (clear). Add Tuno® and continue to sauté for 1 minute while adding cayenne and onion/garlic salt to taste. Turn off heat and pour coconut oil over mixture and stir in well. Cover pan and let sit for a few minutes. Serve with Soppy's Trinidad Coconut Bake (see page 34 for recipe) or bread.

Note: In Trinidad, a similar dish is called Buljol using saltfish.

Jamaican Ackee and "Tuna"

1 can Jamaican ackee (or one dozen fresh)
2 stalks scallion, chopped
¼ cup onion, chopped
¼ cup fresh tomatoes, chopped
1 teaspoon fresh thyme leaves
2 tablespoons coconut oil
1 (12-ounce) roll frozen vegetarian tuna (canned Tuno® may be substituted), thawed and mashed
Pinch of cayenne pepper
½ teaspoon McKay's chicken-style seasoning

Method

Open ackee can and pour into a colander. Rinse under tap water and let drain.

Sauté the scallion, onions, tomatoes, and thyme in the coconut oil.

Add Tuno® and blend well. Add ackee, pepper, and the chicken-style seasoning. Gently stir and allow to simmer for 10–15 minutes.

Note: You may add any vegetarian meat substitute, such as breakfast sausage, if you cannot find frozen vegetarian tuna or Tuno®. Ackee is a great vegan scrambled egg substitute cooked with—or without—any meat analog. Ackee and salted cod fish is the national dish of my home country, Jamaica West Indies. Canned ackee may be found in the ethnic section of most supermarkets. Frozen vegetarian tuna is a great substitute for saltfish.

Fried Dumplings (Floats) 1

2 pounds flour
½ cup fine corn meal
1 package quick rise yeast (or 2¼ teaspoons bulk yeast)
1 tablespoon brown sugar
2 tablespoons vegan butter or margarine
Warm soy milk (enough to make soft dough; start with one cup room temperature milk and add more a little at a time as needed)
Pinch of salt

> ### Method
>
> Place flour, corn meal, yeast, brown sugar, and margarine in a mixing bowl. Add enough warm soy milk to make soft bread dough. Cover with a damp cloth and let rise until double in size.
>
> Pinch off pieces and form into small balls. Roll out each ball with rolling pin and place in frying pan with hot oil.
>
> Fry one at a time in 1½ inches of hot oil over medium heat until dough puffs up.
>
> Flip over and allow other side to get brown.
>
> Make a slit in puffed dumpling and fill with whatever you desire.
>
> *Note:* While dumpling is frying, I use a spoon to gently toss the hot oil over it to help dough to puff quickly.

Fried Dumplings (Floats) 2

4 cups spelt flour
⅓ cup brown sugar
2 tablespoons baking powder
2 tablespoons margarine
¼ teaspoon salt
Warm water

Method

Place all ingredients into a bowl and mix well. Add enough water to make a soft dough. Begin with 2 cups of water and add more a little at a time if needed. Some flour may require more than others.

Cover with damp cloth and allow to rest for 30 minutes. Divide into golf-size balls and allow to rest again for 20 minutes.

Roll out into ¼ inch thick discs and fry in about 1½ inches of hot oil. Fry each side 1–2 minutes.

Frittata

½ cup each of the following vegetables, chopped:
Broccoli
Carrots
Squash
Red pepper
Green pepper
Spinach leaves
Mushrooms
Onion
2 stalks scallion, chopped
1 pound soft tofu
8 ounces vegan cream cheese
½ cup fresh grated coconut
(you may substitute store-bought unsweetened coconut)
1 cup water
1 clove garlic, minced
2 tablespoons nutritional yeast
2 tablespoons coconut oil
Salt and pepper to taste
2 cups shredded vegetarian cheese

Method

In a large glass baking dish, place all vegetables in layers, except crushed garlic.

Purée tofu, cream cheese, coconut, water, nutritional yeast, oil, salt, and pepper in a blender and pour into another bowl. Stir in minced garlic and pour over vegetables. Sprinkle cheese on top and bake at 350 degrees for 45–60 minutes.

Serving suggestion: Enjoy for breakfast, lunch, or dinner with Black Bean Stew (recipe p. 72).

Coconut Yogurt

Meat from 2 young Thai coconuts
One cup coconut water
2 capsules good quality probiotic

Method

Add coconut meat, coconut water, and contents of capsules into strong blender and blend for 45 minutes.

Pour into Mason® glass jar, leaving about one inch space at the top.

Cover with cheese cloth, securing with a rubber band. Place a clean dish cloth over top and place on countertop for 12–24 hours.

Refrigerate for at least 4 hours before eating. Enjoy with honey and berries.

Note: Thai coconuts can be found in all Asian grocery stores, and may also be purchased at most supermarkets in the produce section.

Fruited Yogurt Supreme

½ cup fresh strawberries, diced
½ cup blueberries
½ cup ripe mangoes, diced
½ cup ripe bananas, diced
Desired amount of favorite soy yogurt
¼ cup chopped raw cashews
1 tablespoon chia seeds

Method

Layer fruits into a bowl. Cover with yogurt and sprinkle with cashews and chia seeds.

You may also top with granola if you desire.

Açaí Bowl

½ cup frozen strawberries
½ cup frozen blueberries
¼ cup frozen mangoes or pineapple
1 teaspoon açaí powder
½ cup almond milk, added gradually

Topping:
Slices of ripe banana
Granola of choice
Coconut flakes
Chia seeds
Honey for drizzling

Method

Place frozen ingredients with acai powder in blender, adding milk gradually.

Pour out into a bowl and garnish with topping.

Socca

1 cup garbanzo flour
1 cup warm water
2 tablespoons olive oil
¼ teaspoon fresh rosemary leaves, chopped

Method

Mix all ingredients together well and allow to sit for a few hours. Spread out on a cookie sheet and broil for 5 minutes. Eat with hummus or pesto.

Jamaican Peanut Porridge

1 cup raw peanuts
1 cup oatmeal
1 tablespoon whole wheat flour
1 teaspoon cornmeal
½ teaspoon salt
3 cups very vanilla soy milk or coconut milk
Pinch nutmeg
½ teaspoon vanilla
½ cup brown sugar (less if you desire)

Method

Blend peanuts in a strong blender until almost smooth and pour into a pot. Place oatmeal into same blender and blend into powder. Combine oatmeal, flour, cornmeal, and salt into pot with blended peanuts. Add milk to mixture and whisk to a smooth consistency.

Put on stove and stir until it comes to a boil. Continue stirring as porridge cooks for 5–10 minutes. Remove from stove and add nutmeg, vanilla, and sugar (if desired).

Cornmeal Porridge

3½ cups coconut or soy milk
¾ cup cornmeal
¼ teaspoon nutmeg
½ teaspoon vanilla
1 cinnamon stick or ½ teaspoon cinnamon powder
Brown sugar or sweetener of choice
Pinch of salt (if desired)

Method

Place coconut or soy milk, cornmeal, nutmeg, and vanilla in a medium-sized saucepan and mix well. Bring to boil while constantly stirring. After cornmeal mixture reaches boiling point, allow to simmer for 5–10 minutes. Stir occasionally to avoid lumps from forming. Remove from fire and sweeten to taste. You may add your favorite toppings such as nuts, seeds, bananas, or berries for add nutrition.

Peanut Butter Punch

2 cups soy milk or almond milk
1 large frozen banana
1 heaping tablespoon natural peanut butter
6 whole dates
2 tablespoons rolled oats
1 teaspoon vanilla essence

Method

Place all ingredients into a blender and blend for at least two minutes or until smooth and creamy. Sprinkle with cinnamon powder.

Sparkling Mango Drink

2 cups frozen mango pieces
1 cup orange juice with pulp
¾ cup cold sparkling water
2 tablespoons fresh lime juice
Dash of angostura bitters, optional

Method

Blend all ingredients in a blender until smooth.

Note: Angostura bitters may be found in most ethnic grocery stores or anywhere drink mixture ingredients are found.

Creamy Mango Smoothie

5 cups diced ripe mangos
1 cup nut milk
Condensed milk to taste (see page 45 for Vegan Condensed Milk recipe)
¼ teaspoon rose water flavoring

Method

Place all ingredients in a blender and blend until smooth.
You may add more soymilk or water to make smoothie more diluted if it is too thick.
Note: Food-grade rose water may be found on Amazon or in ethnic grocery stores where vanilla and almond essence are kept.

Strawberry Banana Nog

1 cup fresh strawberries, sliced
1 cup frozen ripe bananas
½ cup plain soy yogurt
2 pitted dates
Dash of nutmeg

Method

Place all ingredients in a blender and blend until smooth.

Piña Colada

1 cup pineapple juice
1 cup almond milk
1 cup orange juice
½ cup coconut milk
1 cup ice cubes

Method

Place all ingredients in a blender and blend well on high.

Vegan Condensed Milk

1¼ cups soymilk powder
¾ cup cane sugar
2 tablespoons unrefined coconut oil
¼ teaspoon sea salt
½ cup hot water

Method

Grind milk powder and sugar with a blender until powdery. Add coconut oil and salt to hot water and pour into blender. Blend until thick and creamy.

Almond Coconut Blend Milk

1 cup almonds, soaked overnight
1 cup fresh coconut pieces
2-4 pitted dates
6 cups distilled water, divided
Pinch of salt

Method

Blend all ingredients in blender with three cups of the water for two minutes. Add remaining water and blend for an additional minute. Strain using a milk bag or cheesecloth and use as a base for smoothies, hot or cold cereals, dressings, soups, etc.

Cashew-Sesame Milk

¾ cup raw cashews
¼ cup sesame seeds
5 cups purified water, divided
3-4 pitted dates
¼ teaspoon salt
¼ teaspoon vanilla extract

Method

Place cashews, sesame seeds, and 2 cups of the water into blender and blend until creamy. Add dates, salt, vanilla extract, and remaining water and whiz until completely blended. Pour out through a cheesecloth or milk bag to strain and squeeze out milk. Chill and serve.

Organic Soybean Milk

2 cups organic soybeans
⅛ teaspoon salt
2 quarts distilled water
Dates
¼ teaspoon vanilla extract

Method

Add beans and salt to the distilled water and bring to a boil. Simmer on low heat for 5-10 minutes. Drain water from beans and allow to cool. Measure beans to see how many cups are available. In a blender, blend each 1 cup of beans to 3 cups of water and 3-4 pitted dates. Flavor with vanilla. Strain through milk bag or cheesecloth and place in refrigerator. This will last up to 5 days in the refrigerator.

Roma® and Banana Latte

2 ripe bananas cut in chunks and frozen over night
½ cup soft Mori-Nu® tofu
1 cup vegan frozen yogurt or ice cream, plain or vanilla
1 cup vanilla soy milk
3 teaspoons Roma® instant grain beverage
1 peppermint stick, crushed, optional
Dash of cinnamon
1 cup ice cubes

Method

Place all ingredients in a strong blender and whiz until smooth.

Note: Roma® is a caffeine-free coffee substitute.

Banana Jackfruit Ice Cream

5 ripe bananas, cut into pieces and frozen
1 cup frozen, ripe jackfruit pieces
Pinch of salt
½ cup almond milk (more or less)

Method

Put ingredients into a blender and blend on high until smooth.

Soy Yogurt

1 package firm Mori-Nu® tofu
Juice from 1 fresh lemon
2 tablespoons coconut oil
2 tablespoons honey + 1 teaspoon honey
½ teaspoon salt

Method

Place all ingredients in a blender and whiz until creamy. Chill overnight and serve with fresh berries.

Strawberry Slush

1 cup fresh organic strawberries, hulled and halved
2 tablespoons sugar
½ cup orange juice
Juice from 1 fresh lemon

Method

Combine all ingredients in a blender or food processor and process until slushy.

Mango Ginger Lassie

2 ripe mangoes
1 inch of fresh ginger
12 ounces vanilla yogurt
2 cardamom seeds
4 dates
1 cup ice

Method

Place all ingredients in a blender and whiz until smooth.

Hot Peppermint Chocolate Drink

4 cups soy milk
1 cup white chocolate, chopped or shaved
½ cup peppermint sticks, ground
½ teaspoon fresh grated nutmeg
Sweetener of choice, if desired

Method

Place milk, chocolate, and peppermint in a saucepan on low heat, and slowly bring to almost boiling point. Keep stirring until chocolate is dissolved (peppermint does not have to be totally dissolved). Add nutmeg and sweetener of choice if desired.

Hot Carob Tea

5 cups coconut milk
¾ cup carob chips
Pinch of cardamom and coriander spice
Sweetener if desired

Method

Place coconut milk in a saucepan over low heat. Add carob and spices into milk and stir as carob melts slowly. Add sweetener if desired.

Whipped Cream

1 cup nut milk
1 cup coconut oil
½ cup evaporated sugar cane crystals
¼ cup fresh lemon juice
½ teaspoon salt

Method

Blend all ingredients in a blender until creamy and fluffy.

Kids' Good Morning Smoothie

1 cup orange juice
1 cup pineapple juice (plant-based milk can be substituted)
1 cup frozen mango
1 frozen ripe banana

Method

Blend all ingredients until smooth. Extra smoothie may be poured into a small zipper sandwich bag and placed in freezer for later use. Make a small opening at one end of plastic bag and allow kids to enjoy frozen treat.

Note: This creates a fun slushie in a bag for kids, with less mess to clean up on floor or clothes.

Morning Goodness Smoothie

½ cup frozen pineapple chunks
½ cup frozen bananas pieces
⅓ cup frozen peaches
3 dates
1⅓ cups plant-based milk

Method

Blend all ingredients until smooth.

Easy Smoothie

1 cup frozen strawberries
1½ cups frozen banana pieces
½ tablespoon chia seeds
3 dates
1 cup coconut milk

Method

Blend all ingredients until smooth.

Immune Booster Smoothie

½ cup frozen blueberries
½ cup pomegranate
½ cup green apple
⅓ cup frozen banana pieces
⅔ tablespoon chia seeds
3–4 dates
1⅓ cups almond milk

Method

Blend all ingredients until smooth.

Tropical Smoothie

1 cup frozen mangos
⅔ cup frozen banana pieces
3–4 dates
1 tablespoon matcha powder
1 tablespoon wheat grass powder
1⅓ cup almond milk

Method

Blend all ingredients until smooth.

Peachy Berry Smoothie

1 cup frozen peaches
1 cup strawberries, washed
1 cup pineapple juice
1 cup plain soy yogurt
1 tablespoon flax seeds
1 cup ice cubes

Method
Blend all ingredients together until smooth.

Super Green Smoothie

1 cup kale
½ cup fresh parsley
1 cup green grapes
1 medium cucumber with skin
1 cup fresh pineapple, peeled and diced
2 cups coconut water

Method

Place kale and parsley into a blender and blend for one minute. Add other ingredients to blender and blend for another 90 seconds. It is important to use a powerful blender for this recipe to ensure that the grape and cucumber skins and the kale are smooth. Less powerful blenders can leave pieces or chunks after blending.

Gentle Greens Smoothie

⅔ cup frozen banana pieces
⅔ cup frozen peaches
½ cup green apples, diced
3 dates
1 tablespoon kale powder
1 tablespoon wheatgrass powder
1⅓ cups plant-based milk

Method

Blend all ingredients until smooth.

Bright Eyes Smoothie

1 medium organic carrot, scrubbed well and cut up
½ cup cantaloupe melon
1 frozen ripe banana
1 cup fortified orange juice
1 teaspoon wheat germ
1 inch of ginger root, peeled

Method

Place ingredients into a sturdy blender (such as a Vitamix® or a Blendtec®) and blend for 2–3 minutes until smooth.

Melon and Ginger Cooler

4 cups melon of choice
3 inches fresh ginger blended in ½ cup water and strained
¼ cup fresh lime juice
Sweetener of choice
Ice cubes

Method

Blend all ingredients in blender until smooth.

Party Punch

2–3-inch piece of fresh ginger root
4 cups pineapple juice
4 cups orange juice
2 quarts apple juice
1 liter ginger ale
Ice cubes

Method

Peel and wash ginger root. Place in a blender with pineapple juice and pulse.

Strain into a large punch bowl and pour in all other items, adding ginger ale last.

Plantain Punch

2 ripe plantains, boiled and cooled
4 cups Very Vanilla Silk® soy milk
2 tablespoons organic peanut butter
1 teaspoon cinnamon
½ teaspoon nutmeg
4–6 dates
Favorite sweetener, optional
Ice cubes

Method

Put all ingredients in blender and blend until smooth and creamy.

Cucumber Drink

5 large unpeeled cucumbers, washed and cut up
3 inches of fresh ginger root, peeled
6–8 cups distilled water
2–3 fresh squeezed limes or lemons
1–2 cups sugar, optional
Ice cubes

> **Method**
>
> Blend cucumbers, ginger root, distilled water, and lime or lemon juice in a blender. Strain through a fine strainer and sweeten if desired.
>
> Serve over ice.

Hawaiian Lemonade for a Crowd

3 cups Country Time® lemonade mix
2 cups sugar, more or less based on desired sweetness
4 cups frozen strawberries, pureed
2 gallons distilled water, more or less for desired taste
Few dashes Angostura® bitters

> **Method**
>
> Pour ingredients into a large container and mix. Taste for sweetness and add more sugar if needed. Enjoy with ice.
>
> Use more or less lemonade mix and sugar for desired tartness.

Spiced Chai Mix

2 ounces ground cinnamon
2 ounces ground cardamom
2 ounces ground allspice
2 ounces ground cloves
2 ounces ground ginger
1 teaspoon grated nutmeg

> **Method**
>
> Mix all ingredients together and store in a glass jar.
>
> *Serving suggestion:* Add 1 teaspoon to 1 cup of hot plant-based milk for a hot drink, or put in a blender with cold milk.

Cold or Hot Chai

1 tablespoon chai mix
1 teaspoon rose water
3 cups brewed herb tea
5 tablespoons honey
1 quart Very Vanilla Silk® soy milk
Ice cubes

Method

Place all ingredients in blender and blend on high for 60 seconds.

FOR HOT CHAI USE HOT SOY MILK AND HAND WISK TO MINIMIZE THE CHANCES OF GETTING BURNED.

Note: Rose water may be purchased on Amazon or in any ethnic grocery store.

Tofu Pero® Latte

1 cup silken tofu
1 cup soy frozen yogurt
1 cup very vanilla soy milk
1 tablespoon Pero® granules (a caffeine-free coffee substitute)
½ teaspoon grated nutmeg
Dash cinnamon

Method

Place all ingredients in a blender and whiz until smooth and creamy. Pour over ice and enjoy.

Note: Pero® is best, but you may use any other coffee substitute.

Beet Drink

4 cups raw beets, chopped
6 cups water
Sugar for sweetening, optional
Juice from 3 fresh squeezed limes
Few drops rose water flavoring (see note in previous cold or hot chai recipe)
Pinch of salt

Method

Blend beets and water in a blender and strain into jug. Add sugar, salt, lime juice, and rose water to the beet water. Stir well and taste. Add more sugar if desired.

Hot Peanut Butter Tea

¼ cup organic peanut butter, more if desired
3–4 cups hot soy milk
Spices and sweetener of choice

Method

Place peanut butter with a small amount of milk in a blender and whiz until smooth and creamy. Add to remainder of hot milk and mix well with spices and sweetener.

Be careful when blending with hot liquids.

Ginger Tea

2 tablespoons fresh ginger root, grated
2–3 cups water
Sweetener of choice

Method

Add ginger to water and bring to boil. Turn off heat and cover pot for 30–60 minutes.

Pour liquid through a strainer into cup and drink with or without sweetener.

Note: You may substitute two tablespoons of fresh rosemary leaves for tea instead of ginger.

Chapter 2

Soups and Stews

Spiritizer

Spiritual Healing

Devotional thought presented for the discussion topic on the Forum at GCE,

"Spiritual Healing."

On page 350 of *The Desire of the Ages*, an amazing book that recounts the life of Jesus, the author draws attention to the fact that during His ministry, Jesus spent more time in healing the sick than preaching.

For many His voice was the first voice heard. His name was the first word spoken. His face was the first face seen.

> *Be healthy, as much as you can and for as long as you can, but don't neglect the spiritual side of health.*

"Now when the sun was setting, all they that had any sick with divers diseases brought them unto him; and he laid his hands on every one of them, and healed them" (Luke 4:40, AKJV).

"Bless the Lord, O my soul, and forget not all his benefits: Who forgiveth all thine iniquities; who heals all thy diseases" (Psalm 103:2-3, KJV).

Physical health and healing are important. We ought to have a good quality of life here on earth. That way our joy would be overflowing, our lives would be more fulfilled, and our ministry would be more effective. But life here on earth has its limits. We age and we die sooner or later. Even the people Jesus healed or raised from the dead died at some later point—even Lazarus.

John said in 3 John 2 (AKJV): "Beloved, I wish above all things that thou mayest prosper and be in health." He then added in the same verse, "even as thy soul prospereth." It would seem here that the prosperity of the soul is of the utmost importance is this statement. Yes, be healthy, as much as you can and for as long as you can, but don't neglect the spiritual side of health. I believe that paramount to physical health and healing is spiritual health and spiritual healing. Where physical healing fails, spiritual healing triumphs.

Yes, God does heal our diseases, and the worst of our diseases is SIN.

Peanut Soup 1

3 cups vegetable broth
1 cup hot water
¾ cup organic peanut butter (feel free to use less if desired)
2 ripe tomatoes, chopped
2 medium carrots, chopped, or 2 cups diced pumpkin
2 garlic cloves, crushed
1 medium onion, finely chopped
1 teaspoon fresh thyme leaves
Salt and pepper to taste

Method

Simmer all ingredients until smooth and creamy. Keep heat low so peanut butter will not burn or scorch. Serve hot over brown rice or a baked potato.

Peanut Soup 2

3 cups vegetable broth
1 cup fresh coconut milk
3 stalks green onions, minced
½ cup green pepper, finely chopped
¼ teaspoon crushed garlic
1 teaspoon fresh thyme leaves
2 tablespoons nutritional yeast
1 pound eddo, peeled and cut in cubes
1 cup carrots or pumpkin, chopped
½ cup potatoes, cubed
1 cup fresh tomatoes, chopped
½ cup organic peanut butter
Salt and pepper to taste

Method

Place all ingredients into a large stock pot and cook slowly on medium heat for 45–60 minutes, stirring frequently.
Serve with crusty bread.
Note: Eddo may be found in most grocery stores in the produce section or in any Caribbean or ethnic grocery store.

Pumpkin and Bean Soup

2 pounds pumpkin, cubed with skin on
4 vegetarian bouillon cubes
2 stalks scallion
6 cups water
2 cups cooked red kidney beans
2 cups fresh squeezed coconut milk
1 teaspoon fresh thyme leaves
¼ cup nutritional yeast
Dash of sea salt (optional)

Method

Place pumpkin, bouillon, and scallion into water and boil until pumpkin is soft, and then add the beans.

Pour small batches into a blender and gently pulse. **Be careful when blending hot liquids**.

Return to pot and add fresh coconut milk.

Stir constantly until soup reaches boiling point, then add thyme leaves, yeast flakes, and salt if desired.

Remove from heat and serve hot.

Spinach Soup

6 cups water
4–6 vegetarian bouillon cubes
2 pounds frozen chopped spinach
2 pounds Jamaican yellow yam, cut in small pieces
2 pounds eddoes, cut in small pieces
3 cups diced kabuca squash, or pumpkin
Spinners (see page 73 for recipe; multiply by three or four times to have enough)
3 stalks scallion, chopped
1 tablespoon fresh thyme leaves
1 package vegetable soup mix
2 cups fresh squeezed coconut milk
Salt to taste

Method

Place large stock pot with water and bouillon cubes on high heat and bring to boiling point.

Carefully place frozen spinach, yam, eddoes, pumpkin and spinners into stock pot.

Cook for 45–60 minutes and then add the scallion, thyme, soup mix, and coconut milk.

Lower heat to medium and cook until yams are soft.

Taste to see if you need to add more salt or seasoning.

Be creative and add your favorite soup seasonings of choice.

Note: Jamaican yellow yam and eddo can be found in most grocery stores in their ethnic section.

Vegetable Bounty Soup

8 cups water
2 pounds pumpkin with skin, cubed
2 medium carrots, coined
2 cups kale, red cabbage, or spinach (you may combine all three)
1 large potato with skin, washed and cubed
1 medium onion, chopped
4 stalks scallion, cleaned and chopped
4 vegetarian bouillon cubes
¼ cup quinoa
½ teaspoon garlic powder
1 teaspoon salt

Method

Bring water to boil into a large soup pot and add all ingredients. Cook for about 45 minutes or until everything is soft. Taste for flavor and add more salt or seasoning if needed.

Note: Pumpkin skin is very nutritious and does not alter the taste of the recipe. However, for those who prefer, you can peel the pumpkin in the recipes in which they are featured.

Lentil Soup

- 8 cups water
- 1 pound lentils, washed
- 1 medium onion, chopped
- 2 stalks celery, chopped
- 4 tablespoons vegetarian beef-style seasoning (more if desired)
- 2 cups fresh spinach
- 2 stalks scallion, chopped
- 1 cup potatoes, diced
- 1 spinners recipe (see page 73 for recipe)
- Salt to taste

Method

Place all ingredients in a stock pot and cook until potatoes and lentils are soft (about 40–60 minutes). Season to taste. Serve with multigrain bread.

Note: Look for and remove small stones and debris from lentils before washing.

15-Bean Soup

7 cups water
1 pack 15-bean soup mix, soaked overnight (discard seasoning packet if included in bag)
3 cups pumpkin, cut into chunks
1 spinners recipe (see page 73 for recipe)
2 cup fresh coconut milk
4 tablespoons vegetarian chicken-style seasoning
3 stalks scallion, chopped
2 teaspoons fresh thyme leaves
3 tablespoons nutritional yeast
Salt to taste

Method

Place beans into a large soup pot with the water and cook for about 40 minutes or until soft.

Add pumpkin, spinners, and all other ingredients and let cook for about another 15–20 minutes. Season to taste.

If soup is not thick enough, remove some of the liquid (including some beans) and blend in a blender until smooth. You may also use an immersion blender and leave soup in the pot. If using traditional blender return to pot and repeat process until desired thickness is achieved. **Be careful when blending hot liquids.**

Note: Soup left over-night will thicken even more. You may use an immersion blender.

Jamaican Red Bean Soup

1 pound kidney beans, soaked overnight, rinsed, and cooked until soft (about 45 minutes)
2 pounds yellow yams, cut into chunks
1 spinners recipe (see page 73 for recipe)
2 pounds pumpkin with skin, cut into pieces
2 large carrots, scrubbed and chopped
4–6 vegetarian bouillon cubes
7 cups water
2 cups fresh coconut milk
3 sprigs fresh thyme
4 whole pimento seeds, optional
¼ cup nutritional yeast
2 stalks scallion, chopped
Salt to taste

Method

Place the kidney beans, yams, spinners, pumpkin, carrots, and bouillon cubes with the water into soup pot and slowly bring to boil. Cook on medium heat until yams pieces are soft, about 30–45 minutes. Add coconut milk, thyme, pimento seeds, nutritional yeast, and scallion and simmer for another 10–20 minutes.

Crockpot Green Split Pea Soup

1 pound split peas, washed
3 cups potatoes, diced
2 cups carrots, diced
10 cups hot water
2 cups coconut milk
1 teaspoon dried thyme leaves
4 stalks scallion, crushed
3 cloves garlic, crushed
4 chicken-style bouillon cubes or 4 teaspoons chicken-style seasoning (add more if needed)

Method

Place all ingredients in a slow cooker and cook on high for 6–8 hours.

Black and Red Bean Soup

½ pound dried red beans, soaked overnight
½ pound dried black beans, soaked overnight
2 quarts water
½ cup fresh coconut, diced
2 tablespoon peanut or cashew butter
2 cups onions, chopped
½ cup red pepper, chopped
1 cup green pepper, chopped
1 teaspoon dried oregano
4 tablespoons nutritional yeast
1 tablespoon fresh thyme leaves
3–4 vegetarian bouillon cubes
Salt and pepper to taste

Method

After soaking, rinse beans in fresh running water and place in a heavy soup pot with the water, salted. Cook beans until soft and mushy, about 45 minutes.

Place 1 cup of liquid from cooked bean with some of the cooked beans in a blender and add diced coconut and peanut butter.

Return pureed contents to the pot with all other ingredients and simmer for 20 minutes.

Cream of Tomato Soup

2 cups ripe tomatoes, diced
1 bay leaf
1 tablespoon nutritional yeast
2 vegetarian bouillon cubes
1 cup water
Cream sauce recipe (see pg. 70 for recipe)

Method

Place all ingredients except cream sauce in saucepan and bring to boil.
Turn off heat and add hot cream sauce.
Pour all ingredients into blender and carefully blend or use an immersion blender.
Use care when blending hot liquids.

Cream Sauce for Cream Soup

2 tablespoons flour
2 tablespoons vegan margarine or coconut oil
2 cups fresh coconut milk or 1½ cans of coconut milk
Salt and white pepper to taste

Method

Melt vegan margarine or coconut oil in saucepan over medium heat. Add flour, salt, and pepper to margarine and quickly whisk with a wire whisk until smooth—do not allow to burn. Slowly add the coconut milk while stirring and cook until thickened.

Note: Use this as the base for any cream soup recipe in this cookbook.

Plantain Balls for Stew or Soup

5 medium green plantains, do not peel
½ teaspoon salt
¼ teaspoon fresh lemon juice
5 cloves garlic, crushed
2 tablespoons coconut oil
Ground pecan or almond meal

Method

Place large pot with salted water on stove on high heat and bring to boil.

Cut off both ends from each plantain, cut in halves, and place into boiling water to cook until soft, about 30 minutes. Remove cooked plantains from pot and allow to cool.

Remove peel from plantains and cut in small pieces and place in bowl.

Add all the other ingredients to the bowl and mash with a fork until mixture is smooth.

Form mixture into golf-size balls and roll in pecan or almond meal to coat.

Plantain balls are great served in stews or bean soup.

Pureed Pumpkin Soup

2 pounds pumpkin with skin, scrubbed and cut into cubes
2 stalks scallion
1 teaspoon fresh thyme leaves
5 cups water or vegetable stock
4 tablespoon vegetarian chicken-style seasoning (adjust seasoning if using stock)
1 cup fresh coconut milk or unsweetened soy milk

Method

Clean scallions and cut in pieces.
Place pumpkin, scallion, and water in stock pot and cook until soft.
Place mixture in blender, or use immersion blender, and thoroughly puree.
Be careful when blending hot liquid.
Return pureed soup to pot and add seasoning.
Bring back to boiling point and slowly add milk.
Stir until soup starts to bubble.
Turn off heat and cover pot; let sit for 10 minutes.
Add more seasoning according to your taste.

Black Bean Stew

1 cup onion, chopped
4 cloves garlic, minced
3 tablespoons coconut oil
1 pound black beans, soaked overnight and rinsed
8 cups water
1 teaspoon fresh thyme leaves
2 tablespoons vegetarian chicken-style seasoning
2 bay leaves

Method

Sauté onions and garlic with oil. Add other ingredients into pot and bring to boil. Turn stove down and allow to cook slowly, about 45–60 minutes. Remove bay leaf. If stew is too thick, add some coconut milk.

Spinners for Soups and Stews

1 cup flour of choice
1 tablespoon corn meal
¼ teaspoon salt
¼–½ cup water

Method

Combine flour with cornmeal and salt and slowly add enough water to make a medium soft dough.

Break off small pieces from dough and gently rub between both hands to form dumplings 2–3 inches long. Add to stews or soups.

Soy Curls with Lentils Stew

½ cup onion, chopped
3 cloves garlic, crushed
1 teaspoon smoked paprika
2 tablespoons oil
1 pound soy curls, rehydrated and drained of water
2–3 vegetarian bouillon cubes, or desired amount of other seasonings
1 pound lentils, washed and cooked in salted water per package directions
1 can coconut milk
1 teaspoon dried thyme leaves

Method

Sauté onions, garlic, and paprika in oil. Add soy curls and bouillon and mix well. Mix in cooked lentils, thyme, and coconut milk to make stew. Simmer on low heat for 10 minutes. If too thick, thin with desired amount of water.

Okra Stew

1 pack frozen cut okra (or 1 pound fresh)
1 teaspoon original all-purpose Spike® seasoning
1 small red onion, diced
1 stalk scallion, chopped
1 tablespoon coconut oil

Method

Place all ingredients into a saucepan. Cover with lid and cook over medium to low heat and allow to slowly steam until soft, about 5–10 minutes (do not add water).

Serve hot as is, or place cooked okra in a food processor and pulse for a coarse chop.

Gluten and Pigeon Peas Stew

1 pound frozen green pigeon peas
4 cups fresh coconut milk or canned coconut milk
1 cup onion, chopped
2 cloves garlic, crushed
1 cup crushed tomatoes, canned or fresh
1 tablespoon fresh thyme leaves
2 tablespoons low salt soy sauce
2 cups carrots, diced
Salt and pepper to taste
2 cups fried chicken-style gluten pieces

Method

Cook pigeon peas with coconut milk until soft, about 30–35 minutes. Add all other ingredients into pot with peas, except gluten and allow to simmer for 20 minutes. Lay gluten pieces on top of contents and continue to simmer for another 10 minutes.

Note: To make fried chicken-style gluten pieces start by cutting up pieces of gluten. Next coat with a flour or breading mix. Fry in hot oil until golden brown.

Chapter 3

Vegetables, Salads and Dressings

Spiritizer

Noise

Devotional thought presented for the discussion topic on the Forum at GCE, **"Noise."**

The wise man Solomon said there is a time and a season for everything under the sun (Eccles. 3:1–4, NIV),

> A time to be born and a time to die,
> A time to plant and a time to uproot,
> A time to kill and a time to heal,
> A time to tear down and a time to build,
> A time to weep and a time to laugh,
> A time to mourn and a time to dance.

I am sure he wouldn't mind if I added: a time to be loud and a time to be soft and low-pitched.

It seems to me that when the Lord wants to proclaim the Good News (the Gospel) of salvation, loudness is appropriate—especially in the last days, loudness is not just appropriate but is desirable, and recommended.

The final message to the world recorded in the 14th chapter of Revelation is to be given with a loud voice. The warning and the queuing of apocalyptic events for the last days are sounded by the seven angels and their seven trumpets in Revelation chapters 8–11.

The psalmist actually promotes, and urges, loudness and jubilance in worship.

Psalm 81:1–2: "Sing for joy to God our strength; shout aloud to the God of Jacob! Begin the music, strike the timbrel, play the melodious harp and lyre" (NIV).

Psalm 95:1–2: "Come, let us sing for joy to the LORD; let us shout aloud to the Rock of our salvation. Let us come before him with thanksgiving and extol him with music and song" (NIV).

Psalm 98:4–6: "Shout for joy to the LORD, all the earth, burst into jubilant song with music; make music to the LORD with the harp, with the harp and the sound of singing, with trumpets and the blast of the ram's horn—shout for joy before the LORD, the King" (NIV).

Said the prophet Zephaniah: "Sing, O daughter of Zion; shout, O Israel; be glad and rejoice with all the heart, O daughter of Jerusalem" (Zeph. 3:14, KJV).

Again, there is a time to be loud. But there is also a time to be soft-spoken, quiet, and even still. When God is peaking to us it's time to be quite and still.

Psalm 46:10: "Be still, and know that I am God" (KJV).

> *When the Holy Spirit speaks to us through our consciences, He does it in a still small voice.*

1 Kings 19:11–12: "And behold, the LORD passed by [Elijah], and a great and strong wind tore into the mountains and broke the rocks in pieces before the LORD, but the LORD was not in the wind; and after the wind an earthquake, but the LORD was not in the earthquake; and after the earthquake a fire, but the LORD was not in the fire; and after the fire a still small voice" (NKJV).

When the Holy Spirit speaks to us through our consciences, He does it in a still small voice.

Isaiah 30:21: "Thine ears shall hear a word behind thee, saying, This is the way, walk ye in it" (KJV).

And so, a loud voice for warning, proclamation, and promulgation, but a still, soft voice for inspiration, motivation, and revelation.

Make no mistake about it though, when all our troubles and trials here are over, and the Father says to Jesus, "Son, go get my children!" there will be no whisper or still small voice, or hush hush about the coming of our Lord for His children.

The Lord will descend from Heaven with a SHOUT and with the voice of the Archangel.

Even so Lord Jesus, come quickly, and loudly. Amen.

Potatoes and Apples

6 medium sweet potatoes, peeled
1½ cups firm apples, sliced
½ cup brown sugar
Dash of cinnamon
4 tablespoons vegan margarine, melted
½ teaspoon salt

Method

Combine sugar, salt, and cinnamon together in a small container.

Boil potatoes until tender and slice in ¼-inch pieces.

Grease glass baking dish and layer sweet potatoes, apple slices, cinnamon-sugar mixture, and margarine.

Repeat until dish is filled with apples as the last item, and sprinkle with cinnamon sugar and margarine.

Bake in oven for 35–45 minutes at 350 degrees.

Curried Cabbage

2 tablespoons unrefined coconut oil
1 large onion, chopped
1 tablespoon curry powder
2 cloves garlic, crushed
¼ cup fresh or canned coconut milk
1 head cabbage, cut in shreds
2 teaspoons vegetarian chicken-style seasoning
¼ teaspoon black pepper
Dash of salt, optional

Method

Heat oil in skillet and add onion, curry, and garlic, and sauté until onions are translucent.

Add coconut milk and bring up to a boil.

Add shredded cabbage and steam, constantly tossing around in pot until most of the liquid has evaporated (do not cover pot). Add the chicken-style seasoning, black pepper, and salt if desired, tossing until evenly distributed.

Glazed Baby Carrots

2 pounds baby carrots
2 tablespoons vegan margarine
1 tablespoon brown sugar
¾ cup apple juice
2 tablespoons soy sauce
1 teaspoon cinnamon

Method

Add all ingredients into a saucepan and bring to a boil. Simmer 5–7 minutes or until all of the liquid is gone.

Mushroom and Water Chestnut Sauté

1 tablespoon olive oil
1 cup mushrooms of choice, sliced
1 cup water chestnuts, sliced
½ cup green pepper, sliced
1 small onion, sliced
1 teaspoon Spike® seasoning
1 teaspoon nutritional yeast

Method

Heat oil in large sauté pan and add mushrooms, water chestnuts, peppers, and onions.

Sauté until onions are cooked. Add seasonings while still on heat and stir well.

Remove from heat and serve over rice.

Spiritizer

My Special Friend

My Special Friend.

They say that it takes one minute to find a special person, one hour to appreciate them, one day to love them, but an entire life to forget them.

I had a special friend when I was young and lived in a relatively poor home. But my special friend did not care. I attended school with multi-patched khaki pants and faded-out khaki shirts. But my special friend did not care.

I went to school barefooted, up to the ninth grade—while most others wore shoes. But my special friend did not care. My special friend moved around in the company of the middle class. I moved around in the company of the rustics of the community; the plain and the simply, the unsophisticated, the poor. But my special friend did not care.

When I started to attend church, I had one pair of pants. They really were not mine. They were my father's. He gave me his pants to wear to church. They were old and heavy; I attended church every other week, hoping that my friends would not notice the same pair of pants worn every time.

But my special friend seemed not to notice; my special friend did not care. I like friends like those.

>You see friends smile at you, they like your face,
>They want to be with you at any old place.
>Friends have fun with you, friends share;
>They are glad when you are happy, when you are sad that's when they care.
>I got up one morning and looked in the mirror.
>I said to my special school day friend, "I am getting old; I see wear and tear."
>She said, "I still love you, so I really don't care."

> Yes, my childhood friend became my wife.
> There were battles fought with all our might,
> And doors got slammed instead of closed,
> But in the end friends again,
> And that's what count the most.
>
> Through thick and thin, tested by time,
> Our friendship now is in its prime.
> We might grow old, all secrets told,
> But our friendship won't go cold,
> And it's still as gold.

And would you believe that there is even a better and closer friend that I know? The chorus says it this way:

> Closer than a brother my Jesus is to me.
> He's my dearest friend, in everything I need.
> He's my rock, my shield and hiding place.
> Closer than a brother Jesus is to me.

Jesus is my Creator, my Savior, Redeemer, and Forever Friend. Will you make Him your special Friend, too?

Garbanzo Bean Salad

1 (15-ounce) can garbanzo beans, rinsed and coarsely chopped
⅓ cup mayonnaise of choice
¼ cup dried spinach flakes
⅓ cup dried cranberries
¼ cup sunflower seeds
1 teaspoon dill
1 tablespoon nutritional yeast

Method

Gently combine all ingredients in a bowl and use to make sandwiches.

Note: Dried spinach flakes can be found on Amazon or in Amish or health food stores.

Beet and Carrot Salad

2 cups beets, shredded
3 cups carrots, shredded
1 cup raisins or Craisins®
1 cup red cabbage, shredded
2 tablespoons mayonnaise of choice

Method

Place all ingredients in a salad bowl and gently toss until mayonnaise is evenly distributed.

Refrigerate and chill for 1 hour before serving.

B.A.T. (Beans, Avocados, Tomatoes) Salad

1 head red lettuce, washed and dried
2 ripe firm avocados, diced
2 firm ripe red tomatoes, diced
2 firm ripe yellow tomatoes, diced
1 (15.5-ounce) can dark kidney beans, rinsed and drained
2 (15.5-ounce) cans white beans, rinsed and drained
2 teaspoons fresh lemon juice
4 teaspoons extra virgin olive oil
2 teaspoons Bragg® liquid aminos

Method

Chop lettuce very fine and make a nest on a large platter.

Layer avocados, tomatoes, and beans on lettuce nest.

Mix lemon juice, olive oil, and liquid aminos in a small bowl for salad dressing.

Drizzle dressing over salad and serve right away.

Waldorf Salad

2 cups green apples with skin on, chopped
2 cups red grapes cut in halves, seeds removed
2 (8.25-ounce) cans mandarin orange segments, drained
1 cup frozen pineapple/orange juice concentrate
1 cup vanilla Silk® soy yogurt, or cashew cream (see page 23 for recipe)
¼ cup water chestnuts
1 tablespoon poppy seeds, optional
¼ cup celery, chopped, optional

Method

Mix everything in a large bowl. Cover and refrigerate before serving.

Celery Salad

2 stalks celery, finely chopped
1 cup raisins
1 cup watercress
1 cup canned mandarin orange segments, drained
1 cup raw pumpkin seeds
2 tablespoons vegan mayonnaise or mayonnaise of choice (see page 142 for recipe)

Method

Place all ingredients in a salad bowl and toss well. Serve immediately.

Salad in a Bag

1 cup cooked grains, such as Kamut or barley
1 handful chopped red and green cabbage
½ cup cooked black beans
½ cup cooked garbanzo beans
¼ cup golden corn
¼ cup black olives, chopped
1 cup marinated tofu cubes or 1 cup alternative vegetarian meat

Method

Place all ingredients into a large plastic zipper bag and toss well. Add your favorite homemade creamy dressing.

Note: Dice tofu and marinate overnight in your favorite sauce. See recipe for Easy Salad Dressing or Marinade on p. 87.

Mango Salsa

1 large ripe mango, peeled and diced
¼ cup red onion, minced
2 tablespoons lemon juice
1 tablespoon fresh cilantro, minced
¼ teaspoon salt

Method

Combine all ingredients in a bowl and refrigerate until ready to use.
Serve with corn chips.

Sweet Potato Salad

4 cups washed spinach leaves
1 cup raw sweet potato, peeled then shredded
1 cup grape tomatoes
1 whole yellow bell pepper, cut in strips

Method

Place all ingredients in a salad bowl and toss well with favorite dressing.

Green Banana Salad

3 cups boiled green cooking bananas, diced
1 small red onion, finely minced
½ cup green bell pepper, diced
½ cup red bell pepper, diced
½ cup vegan mayonnaise
3 tablespoons nutritional yeast
1 teaspoon fresh parsley, chopped
2 teaspoons vegetarian chicken-style seasoning

Method

Place diced bananas, onions, and peppers in a mixing bowl.
Mix mayonnaise, nutritional yeast, parsley, and chicken-style seasoning in a small container.
Gently fold mixture into bananas, onions, and peppers.
Spoon banana salad into a serving bowl; cover and chill for 2 hours, or overnight.

Layered Potluck Salad

2 cups blue corn chips, crushed
2 cups romaine lettuce, finely shredded
2 cups ripe tomatoes, diced
2 cups green bell pepper, diced
2 cups red bell pepper, diced
2 cups ripe avocados, diced
2 cups red cabbage, finely shredded
2 cups carrots, shredded
2 cups canned sweet green peas, rinsed and drained
½ cup red onions, diced, optional
2 (15.5-ounce) cans red kidney beans, rinsed and drained
½ cup raw pumpkin seeds
½ cup raw sunflower seeds
Zesty Italian dressing

Method

Layer each ingredient as listed into a deep glass salad bowl.
Drizzle dressing over top generously. Refrigerate overnight.

Tofu and Dill Weed Dressing

¼ cup soft tofu
¼ cup vegetarian broth
1 tablespoon apple cider vinegar
1 tablespoon dill
2 garlic cloves, crushed
½ teaspoon Dijon mustard
2 tablespoons extra virgin olive oil
Sea salt to taste, optional

Method

Place tofu, broth, vinegar, dill, garlic, mustard, and salt in a blender and blend.

While blender is running, open the top and slowly pour in olive oil until mixture is smooth.

Raspberry Dressing

3 tablespoons raspberry vinegar
3 tablespoons seedless raspberry jam
¼ cup canola or olive oil

Method

Place vinegar and jam into blender and blend.
While blender is still running, slowly pour in oil until dressing becomes smooth.

Easy Salad Dressing or Marinade

6 tablespoons olive oil
2 tablespoons apple cider vinegar
2 teaspoons Dijon mustard
2 teaspoons lemon juice
¼ teaspoon sea salt
Pinch dried herbs of choice

Method

Whisk all ingredients together in a bowl and pour over salad or use as a marinade for tofu.

Poppyseed Dressing for Fruit Salad

1 cup honey
¼ teaspoon salt
½ teaspoon Dijon mustard
½ cup apple cider vinegar
1 teaspoon poppy seeds

Method

Blend well in a bowl and drizzle over fruit salad.

Sunny Isles Salad Dressing

Juice of one freshly squeezed lemon
1 teaspoon Italian seasoning
1 clove garlic, crushed
½ cup olive oil
Dash of cayenne pepper, optional
Salt to taste

Method

Place ingredients in a glass bottle. Cover bottle and shake well. Place in the refrigerator for 15–30 minutes before using.
Serving Suggestion: For an even more exotic taste, add 1 or 2 tablespoons of peanut butter and a teaspoon of honey and blend in a blender.

Zesty Caribbean-Italian Dressing

Juice of one freshly squeezed lemon
1 cup extra virgin olive oil
1 tablespoon Italian seasoning
1 teaspoon dried oregano
¼ cup Bragg® liquid aminos (more if desired)
1 or 2 tablespoons honey (optional, but very desirable)
½ teaspoon cayenne pepper
Dash of garlic powder, onion powder, or salt

Method

Place all ingredients into a medium-sized glass bottle, cover and shake vigorously for about 1 minute. Place in refrigerator for a couple hours or overnight to allow flavors to be released.

Chapter 4

Entrees

Spiritizer

Money

Devotional thought presented for the discussion topic on the Forum at GCE, "Money."

God is good. His mercy is everlasting, and His grace is AMAZING! No wonder the song says: "Amazing grace how sweet the sound that saved a wretch like me."

You know, it is said that of the thirty-eight parables of Jesus recorded in the New Testament, sixteen of them pertain to the handling of money and our possessions (our finances). Sixteen of thirty-eight—that is 42%.

They say there are over 500 verses on PRAYER, and just under 500 verses on FAITH; yet they say you can find up to 2,000 verses on money and possessions in the whole Bible. This tells me that we ought to think soberly and act prudently and judiciously in the area of our finances.

Here is a quotation from Ellen White in the book *My Life Today*, page 121:

> Money has great value, because it can do great good. In the hands of God's children it is food for the hungry, drink for the thirsty, and clothing for the naked. It is a defense for the oppressed and a means of help to the sick. But money is of no more value than sand … if it is not put to use in providing for the necessities of life, in blessing others, and in advancing the cause of Christ.

As we focus on our finances, and just about everything that relates to it, it is our hope that we will become better stewards relative to our accounts and the blessings we've been given.

Mushroom and Soya Chunks Burgers

2 large portabella mushrooms, chopped
1 large onion, chopped
1 (8-ounce) pack soya vegetarian chunks, soaked and drained
1 cup quick oatmeal
1 cup carrots, shredded
½ cup green onions, chopped
2 tablespoons nutritional yeast
2 tablespoons soy sauce
1 tablespoon vegetarian chicken-style seasoning
1 pound soft tofu, pureed
3 garlic cloves, minced
½ cup warm water

Method

Sauté mushrooms and onions without oil and place into a bowl.
Add all other listed ingredients into the bowl with mushrooms and onions and mix thoroughly.
Leave mixture in bowl covered on counter for 30–60 minutes.
Form into burgers and fry with a little oil until brown on both sides.
Place on a cookie sheet and bake at 350 degrees for 20 minutes.

Peppered Gluten Strips

2 ponds prepared gluten, cut in strips
¼ tablespoon ginger, finely chopped
3 stalks scallion, chopped
4 cloves garlic, chopped
1 tablespoon soy sauce
1 teaspoon salt
1 large green bell pepper, cut in strips
3 tablespoons oil
½ cup canned pineapple chunks
1 tablespoon cornstarch
1¼ cups vegetable stock

Method

In a large bowl, place the gluten, ginger, scallion, garlic, soy sauce, and salt.

Gently mix ingredients together and let sit for a few hours, or overnight in the fridge.

Next day, remove gluten from fridge.

Sauté green peppers in oil and remove from frying pan.

Place gluten in same pan and stir until brown.

Return peppers to pan with remaining marinade and add pineapple chunks.

Mix cornstarch with stock or water and add to pot.

Cook until sauce gets thick. Serve over cooked rice.

Potatoes with Tomato Sauce

1 medium onion, chopped
2 cloves garlic, minced
2 stalks scallion, chopped
2 tablespoons coconut oil
1 can diced or crushed tomatoes
1 tablespoon vegetarian chicken-style seasoning
1 teaspoon dried oregano leaves
Salt and pepper to taste

2 pounds small red potatoes, parboiled and drained
1 cup shredded vegan cheese

Method

Sauté onion, garlic, and scallion with oil in a large skillet over medium heat. Add tomatoes, chicken-style seasoning, oregano, salt, and pepper. Place parboiled potatoes into an 8x8 glass baking dish and pour tomato mixture over top of potatoes. Cover with foil and bake in oven for 30–40 minutes at 350 degrees. Remove from oven and sprinkle with shredded cheese.

Pie in a Ramekin

2 tablespoons oil
1 medium red onion, chopped
1 small red bell pepper, diced
1 small green bell pepper, diced
½ cup canned green peas
1 bunch baby spinach, washed and drained
½ cup sweet corn kernels
2 tablespoons vegetarian chicken-style seasoning
4 tablespoons nutritional yeast
4 vegetarian sausages, minced
1 cup cooked bulgur wheat
1 large eggplant
2 large carrots
½ cup pureed Mori-Nu® firm tofu
1 cup vegan cheddar cheese
Salt and pepper to taste

Method

Grease 1 large ramekin dish and set aside.
Heat oil and sauté onions and peppers.
Stir in peas, spinach, and corn.
Add chicken-style seasoning and turn off heat.
Mix with bulgur and set aside.

With a potato peeler, strip long thin ribbon strips from the eggplant and drop in salted boiling water for 3 minutes.
Remove from water and let drain on paper towel.
Strip long thin ribbons from the carrots.
Line the ramekin dish with the eggplant and carrot ribbons overlapping alternatively, leaving enough over the edge to fold over and cover the top of pie when completed.
Start layering bulgur mixture and vegetable mixture into lined ramekin.
Add nutritional yeast, salt, and pepper to pureed tofu and pour over entire contents in ramekin.
Cover dish by gently bringing all overlapping ribbons to the center.
Place dish in a deep roasting dish or pan and fill halfway up with boiling water.
Cover roasting dish with foil and place in oven preheated to 350 degrees for 30–45 minutes.
Remove from oven and let sit for 5–10 minutes.
Turn out onto platter so pie is upside down.

Tamale

1 cup soft-cooked brown rice
5 medium tomatoes, diced
5 stalks green onions, chopped
1 can sweet green peas
5 cloves of garlic, minced
3 cups minced gluten steaks
2 teaspoons adobo seasoning
3 threads saffron, or 1 teaspoon powdered saffron
2 tablespoons olive oil
4 medium potatoes
4 medium carrots
Salt, pepper and cumin to taste
Banana leaves to wrap tamale (*found in the freezer section of most grocery stores that carry ethnic foods*). If you cannot find any, use foil lined with parchment paper.

Method

<u>The night before</u>: Make a salsa with the tomatoes, onions, green peas, and garlic and refrigerate overnight. Then, season the minced gluten with the adobo, saffron, and oil and let marinate overnight in the refrigerator as well. Finally, wash and cut the banana leaves and let them sit until morning.

<u>In the morning</u>: Peel the potatoes and carrots and cut them in round slices. Mix with the seasoned gluten filling and cook together until potatoes and carrots are soft.

Open the prepared banana leaves and place the rice and gluten filling on it, then carefully fold into tamale and tie it firmly with string.

Place tamale in boiling water and let cook for 15 minutes or until it feels firm to the touch, indicating tamale is cooked. Serve with the salsa.

Baked Burrito

1 teaspoon olive oil
1 large onion, chopped
1 cup tomato, chopped
¼ cup green bell pepper, chopped
1 (10.5-ounce) can low sodium cream of mushroom soup
¼ cup water
2 (15.5-ounce) cans black beans, rinsed and drained
Dash of oregano
Pinch of fresh ground black pepper
1–2 vegetarian bouillon cubes
Pinch of turmeric
6–8 whole wheat tortillas, kept warm

Method

Heat oil and sauté onions, tomatoes, and peppers. Add cream of mushroom soup, bouillon cubes, and ¼ cup water. Add black beans, oregano, and black pepper.

> Cover skillet and simmer for 10 minutes, or until mixture thickens. Spoon ingredients onto each tortilla and fold into burrito. Place burritos into a glass dish with seam side down. Pour any leftover sauce over them and bake covered for 15–25 minutes at 350 degrees, or until slightly brown.

TVP Curry

2 cups dry "beef style" TVP, soaked overnight
1 large onion, chopped
4 cloves garlic, minced
3 stalks green scallion, chopped
5 vegetarian bouillon cubes
1 tablespoon curry powder
¼ cup nutritional yeast
½ cup carrots, shredded
1 can full cream of coconut milk (more if needed)
¼ cup garbanzo flour
Salt as needed
Oil

> ### Method
> Put all ingredients into stock pot together and allow to cook for 45 minutes on low heat.

Rainbow Haystacks

1 medium onion, chopped
1 tablespoon jalapeño peppers, chopped, optional
1 tablespoon coconut oil
2 (15-ounce) cans vegetarian chili (you may use your homemade chili)
2 (15-ounce) cans black or red beans, rinsed and drained
Corn chips, broken into small pieces
1 cup cooked brown rice
2 heads green lettuce, finely shredded
1 firm ripe avocado, diced
2 firm ripe tomatoes, diced

1 cup mixed red, yellow, and orange bell peppers, diced
1 cup black olives, chopped
Shredded vegan cheese

Method

Sauté onions and jalapeño peppers in oil. Add chili and beans. Simmer for 5–10 minutes.

Assemble haystack on plate stacked in this order: corn chips, rice, lettuce, avocado, tomatoes, peppers, olives, and cheese.

Pour hot chili over stack and enjoy.

You may substitute spinach leaves for lettuce.

Oatmeal Meatballs

1 pound firm tofu, mashed
4 cups quick oats
½ cup green bell pepper, diced
1 cup onion, chopped
1 cup walnut meal
3 packages golden George Washington broth mix
1 cup vegan cheddar cheese
1 teaspoon oregano
Salt to taste
Plain coconut milk (if needed for moisture)
Extra cheese

Method

Using your hand, mix all ingredients together, ensuring that tofu and oats are well blended. Add some coconut milk if needed to hold all ingredients together. Make into small golf size balls and bake at 350 degrees for 30 minutes.

Place in a glass dish and pour your favorite sauce to cover over baked meatballs, sprinkle with more cheese and bake until bubbly.

Onion Tofu Loaf

1 pound firm tofu, mashed
½ loaf multi-grain bread, torn in small pieces
1 large onion, minced
1 cup green bell pepper, finely chopped
2 cloves fresh garlic, minced
1 cup pecan meal
1 package dry onion soup mix
½ cup nutritional yeast
2 (10.5-ounce) cans cream of mushroom soup
½ stick melted margarine
Quick oats if needed

Method

Mix all ingredients and form a loaf. If mixture is too wet, add some additional quick oats.

Mixture should not be too wet or too stiff and dry. Bake in a glass loaf pan at 350 degrees for 1 hour.

Apricot Chickett®

4 small Loma Linda Chickett® rolls, thawed and broken into bite size pieces
2 cups low-sugar apricot preserves
2 bottles thousand island dressing
½ cup ketchup

Method

Fry Chickett® pieces in hot oil until golden brown and place in a glass baking dish.

Mix together preserves, dressing, and ketchup.

Pour sauce over Chickett® pieces and place in oven at 350 degrees and bake for 30 minutes, or until brown and glossy.

Note: You may substitute fried gluten pieces for the Chickett®. See following recipe.

Apricot Glazed Gluten

2 pounds chicken-style fried gluten
1 (12-ounce) jar low sugar apricot preserves
2 cups thousand island dressing
½ cup ketchup

Method

Arrange gluten into a deep glass baking dish. In a bowl, mix preserves, dressing, and ketchup thoroughly. Pour sauce over gluten, making sure all pieces are coated.

Place in oven at 350 degrees and bake for 20–30 minutes, or until sauce is brown and gluten has a nice glaze.

Cottage Cheese Nut Loaf

3 cups large curd cottage cheese
2 cups raw cashews, finely chopped
1 cup onion, minced
1 tablespoon fresh garlic, minced
½ cup raw white potato, peeled then shredded
2 cups cubed and toasted bread pieces
½ cup nutritional yeast
1 tablespoon tarragon
1 tablespoon Spike® seasoning
1 tablespoon flax seed

Method

Mix all items together and place in a glass 9x13-inch dish and bake for 1 hour at 350 degrees.

Special K® Roast

½ cup onion, chopped
2 cloves garlic, crushed
4 tablespoons melted vegan margarine

4 cups Kellogg's Special K® cereal
1 pound firm tofu, mashed
1 cup unsweetened nut milk
1½ cups walnuts or pecans
2 tablespoons vegetarian beef-style seasoning
Ener-G® egg replacer for equivalent of 4 eggs

Method

Sauté onions and garlic in margarine. Add the onions and garlic to a large bowl with other ingredients, mix well, and bake at 350 degrees for one hour.

Eggplant Bake

4 eggplants, sliced in ¼ inch pieces
½ cup onion, chopped
½ cup tomato, chopped
2 tablespoons olive oil
1 teaspoon garlic powder
1 cup grated vegan cheddar cheese
¼ cup almond slivers
1–2 tablespoons vegetarian chicken-style seasoning

Method

Sauté eggplant slices with onions and tomatoes until soft. Add other ingredients and mix well.
Pour contents into a glass baking dish and bake at 350 degrees for 20–30 minutes.

Vegetarian Baked Beans

1 cup onions, chopped
1 cup green bell peppers, chopped
2 tablespoons unrefined coconut oil
2 cups cooked northern or pinto beans
2 cups cooked lima beans
2 cups diced or stewed tomatoes

2 tablespoons vegan Worcestershire sauce
6 tablespoons brown sugar
¼ cup molasses
2 tablespoons liquid smoke
1 teaspoon salt
1 tablespoon fresh thyme leaves
1 teaspoon red pepper flakes, optional

Method

Heat oil into a large skillet on medium heat and sauté onions and peppers until tender.
Place all the other ingredients in the skillet and allow to simmer on low heat for 40–60 minutes.

Nut Meat Balls

1 cup pecans
1 cup walnuts
2 cups fresh whole wheat breadcrumbs
1 medium onion, chopped
1–2 pounds tofu, pureed
2 cups vegan cheddar cheese
½ cup nutritional yeast
2 tablespoons vegetarian chicken-style seasoning
1 jar spaghetti sauce

Method

Place all ingredients into food processor, except spaghetti sauce.
Pulse processor a few times to get a coarse chop of ingredients.
Form mixture into meatballs and place on a greased baking sheet.
Bake for 30 minutes at 350 degrees.
Remove meat balls from baking sheet and place into a deep baking dish.
Pour spaghetti sauce over meat balls in dish and bake for an additional 10–20 minutes, or until bubbly.

Mushroom Roast

1 cup portabella mushrooms, chopped
1 cup onion, chopped
1 tablespoon oil
1 cup gluten, ground
2 cups raw potatoes with skin, shredded
1 cup pureed tofu
½ cup instant oatmeal
½ cup nutritional yeast
1 teaspoon vegetarian chicken-style seasoning
3 envelopes golden George Washington broth
1 cup vegan sour cream

Method

Sauté mushrooms and onions with a little oil. Place the mushrooms and onions with the other ingredients in a large bowl and mix thoroughly. Place in a loaf pan and leave on counter for 30 minutes. Bake at 350 degrees for 1 hour.

Quiche

1 large onion, chopped
2 cloves garlic, minced
2 medium-sized tomatoes, chopped and drained of juice
1 tablespoon coconut oil
1 cup chopped vegetarian breakfast sausage crumbles
1 cup vegan shredded pepper jack cheese
1 tablespoon fresh basil, chopped
2 packages soft tofu
1 cup canned coconut milk
2 tablespoons corn starch
½ teaspoon salt
¼ teaspoon freshly ground black pepper
1 prepared flaky pastry shell

Method

Sauté onion, garlic, and tomatoes with oil.
Blend tomato mixture, sausage crumbles, cheese, and basil and pour into pastry shell.
Puree tofu with milk, cornstarch, salt, and pepper.
Pour tofu mixture into pastry shell over contents.
Bake at 350 degrees for 45–60 minutes.
Serving Suggestion: You may substitute any chopped vegetarian meat of choice.

Stewed Gluten

1 cup onion, chopped
3 tablespoons oil
½ cup salted peanuts
1 cup vegetable stock
1 cup water
1 tablespoon vegetarian beef-style seasoning
1 teaspoon fresh thyme leaves
¼ teaspoon black pepper
2 cups crushed tomatoes
1 hot pepper, chopped, optional
2½ cups seasoned and fried gluten pieces

Method

Sauté onions in oil. Rough chop peanuts with stock for 30 seconds into blender.

Add all ingredients into stock pot (except for gluten) and let simmer slowly over low heat for 5 minutes. Add gluten pieces and continue to simmer for 5 more minutes.

Serve over hot jasmine rice.

Redi-burger® Red Top Roast

1 medium onion, chopped
¼ cup canola oil
3 raisin bagels, crumbled in a food processor
1 cup pecan pieces
1 (19-ounce) can Worthington Redi-burger®
2 cup vegan cheddar cheese
1 pound tofu, pureed
3 tablespoons nutritional yeast
1 teaspoon each of onion and garlic powder, and seasoning salt to taste
⅓ cup water
⅓ cup brown sugar
⅓ cup ketchup

Method

Sauté onions in oil then add the bagel crumbs and pecan pieces into skillet and stir.

Mix the Redi-burger®, cheese, tofu, nutritional yeast, onion and garlic powder, and seasoning salt together.

Add the contents from skillet to the burger mixture and pour into a greased glass 9x13-inch dish. Make the glaze by mixing the water, sugar, and catsup, and pour over top of roast.

Bake at 375 degrees for 40–60 minutes or until bubbly and brown on top.

Pecan Meatballs

1 pound firm tofu, mashed
½ cup pecan meal
1 cup old fashioned oats
3 tablespoons vegetarian chicken-style seasoning
2 cups vital wheat gluten flour
¾ cup nutritional yeast
2 tablespoons onion powder
1 tablespoon garlic granules
1 teaspoon sage
1 tablespoon basil
1 cup water

For sauce:
6 cups spaghetti sauce
6 cups water
1 stick vegan margarine
⅓ cup nutritional yeast

Method

Combine sauce ingredients and allow to slowly simmer for 10 minutes then turn off heat.

Mix all of the other ingredients and roll into desired size of meatballs.

Brown meatballs in coconut oil. Add to sauce and bring back up to simmer.

Put mixture in a 9x13-inch glass baking dish if not using an oven-safe sauté pan and bake at 350 degrees for 1½ hours until sauce thickens.

Serve on hoagie bread for meatball subs, or over cooked pasta.

Meatless Roast

½ cup onion, chopped
1 tablespoon oil
2 raisin bagels, crumbled
4 cups rehydrated TVP
1 sleeve saltine crackers, crushed
2 tablespoons vegetarian beef-style seasoning
Replacement (such as Enger-G® brand) for 4 eggs
½ cup nut milk
½ cup ketchup

Method

Sauté onions in oil until transparent, then add crumbled bagels. Mix with all the other ingredients and pour into a loaf pan.

At this point you may combine an additional ½ cup ketchup and ½ cup brown sugar to make a glaze. Spread on top of loaf and bake at 350 degrees for about 1 hour.

Jeremy's Company Roast

1 loaf wheat bread
1 (48-ounce) can Worthington Vege-burger®
⅓ cup olive oil
Seasoning of choice

For Sauce:
1 cup ketchup
1 cup brown sugar (less if desired)
1 cup water

Method

Preheat oven to 375 degrees. Mince the loaf of bread into food processor until the texture is fine like powder. If you don't have a blender or food processor, just strip the slices of bread by hand to the smallest size possible.

In a large bowl, combine the burger, oil, and seasoning with the minced bread. Mix it very well until it binds. (If you can pick it with your hands without it crumbling, that means it's mixed well). Pour the loaf mixture into a greased 9x13-inch baking pan.

Sauce: Mix the ketchup, sugar, and water. Stir until the sugar is completely dissolved, then pour the mixture on top of the loaf evenly.

Bake for 45 minutes, or until the sauce mixture forms a dark glaze and is no longer watery. Remove from oven and allow to rest for about 15–20 minutes for best results.

Rainy Day Pakasa

4 cups fresh coconut milk
2 stalks scallion, chopped
1 medium onion, chopped
1 teaspoon fresh thyme leaves
1 whole scotch bonnet pepper
2 pounds yellow yam, peeled and cut in pieces
2 green plantains, peeled and cut in 3-inch pieces
3–4 vegetarian bouillon cubes
1 teaspoon seasoning salt
½ teaspoon black pepper

Method

Place all ingredients into a heavy saucepan on medium heat and cook until food is soft and almost all the liquid has evaporated. If more liquid is needed to cook yam and plantain, feel free to add more milk.

Note: In the summertime neighborhood kids would come together and cook this dish. You may add spinners and substitute any root food you like.

Entrees ◆ 107

Green Banana/Plantain with Stuffing

16 ounces frozen chopped spinach (thawed and drained)
8 ounces shredded cheddar cheese or cream cheese
5 green bananas/plantains
¼ teaspoon fresh ground pepper
¼ cup green onions, chopped
1 teaspoon fresh thyme leaves
1 small jalapeño, diced, optional
Coconut oil for frying
Salt to taste

Method

Mix together spinach and cheese. Boil bananas/plantains in salted water.
Take plantains out of pot and mash well with a pestle (the bottom of a clean glass bottle is a good substitute). Season with fresh ground pepper, green onions, thyme leaves, and jalapeño peppers. Scoop up enough to make a soft ball size.
Make a well in the center and fill with cheese and spinach.
Seal hole to cover filling and fry until golden brown.
Serve hot with any entrée or peanut soup.

Tofu Cutlets

1 cup seasoned breadcrumbs
2 tablespoons nutritional yeast
½ cup ground walnuts
1 tablespoon dried mixed herbs
2 tablespoons vegetarian chicken-style seasoning
1 pound extra firm tofu, drained
¼ cup soy sauce

Method

Add together breadcrumbs, yeast flakes, ground nuts, herbs, and chicken-style seasoning into one bowl.

Cut tofu block into two triangles then cut each triangle into ¼-inch slices. Sprinkle soy sauce over tofu ensuring that all sides are well coated.

Gently press tofu slices into dry ingredients to coat each side. Spray a cookie sheet with cooking spray and place each slice on sheet close to each other.

Spray top of tofu with spray and place cookie sheet into oven. Bake at 350 degrees until tofu slices are slightly brown on both sides (no need to turn during cooking).

Serving suggestion: These slices make delicious sandwiches.

Rice Krispies® Loaf

1 large onion, chopped
½ cup green bell pepper, chopped
1 stick melted margarine
12 ounces Rice Krispies® cereal
2 pints cottage cheese (nondairy if you can find it)
2 pounds soft tofu, pureed
5 packages golden George Washington broth
1 cup sunflower seeds
Salt and pepper to taste

Method

Sauté onion and pepper with the margarine.

Place all ingredients into a large bowl and thoroughly mix together.

Pour into a greased 9x13-inch glass baking dish and bake for 1 hour at 350 degrees.

Mock Fish

1 pound yellow split peas, soaked overnight
1 dry coconut, broken with white part removed from hard brown shell

¾ cup warm water
2 sheets roasted seaweed (nori)
1 bunch fresh chives
1 bunch fresh thyme
1 stalk celery
2 stalks fresh parsley
3 stalks scallion, chopped
1 large onion, chopped
2 cloves garlic, crushed
2 tablespoons wheat flour
Salt and pepper to taste
½ cup nutritional yeast
½ pound tofu, pureed
Juice from 1 fresh lime
6 large dasheen leaves

Method

Rinse peas in cold water and drain.
In a blender, blend coconut with the warm water to expel milk. Strain blended mixture through a cheese cloth or fine mesh strainer.
Grind split peas in food processor with the coconut milk, seaweed, chives, thyme, celery, parsley, scallion, onions and garlic.
Pour mixture out into a large mixing bowl.
Mix flour into pea mixture, and season to taste with salt, pepper, and nutritional yeast.
Add tofu and lime juice into mixture and thoroughly mix.
Wash dasheen leaves and remove stems.
Place the mixture into leaves and fold like a burrito.
Repeat process until you have 5 or 6 burritos.
Steam for 20–30 minutes in a steamer.
Remove from steamer and let cool.
Slice each roll into ¼-inch fish pieces, and dip into a batter.
Fry until golden brown.
Note: Dasheen leaves may be found in most Caribbean stores. Also, the fiber that is left after expelling milk from coconut may be used to add more flavor and texture to plant-based burgers, cakes, and cookies.

Tortilla Pot Pie

1 cup potatoes, diced
1 cup carrots, diced
1 stick margarine
1 medium onion, chopped
2 stalks celery, chopped
½ cup wheat flour
2½ cups vegetable or chicken-style broth
1 teaspoon kosher salt
½ teaspoon black pepper
Pinch of saffron threads, optional
1 cup corn kernels
2 tablespoons nutritional yeast
1 cup chopped vegetarian meat of choice
1 cup cottage cheese
1 cup canned green peas
Tortillas for layering in a 9x13-inch glass dish

Method

Spray one side of each tortilla with cooking spray and line a deep 9x13-inch glass dish with sprayed side down, overlapping to form a pie shell. Leave a few tortillas for top of pie.

Cook potatoes and carrots for 5 minutes in a saucepan. Sauté onions and celery in margarine.

Mix flour into sautéed ingredients and cook for 3 minutes on low heat stirring constantly until creamy. Whisk as you slowly add stock, salt, pepper, and saffron, and then simmer for a few minutes. Mix in all remaining ingredients and pour into tortilla-lined glass dish.

Cover mixture with remaining tortilla wraps making sure to fold all sides into dish.

Spray the top and bake in oven at 275 degrees for 30–40 minutes or until brown on top.

Dinner Roast Pot Pie

1½ cups carrot, coined
1½ cups potatoes, diced
1⅓ cups water, divided
2 cups mushrooms, chopped
½ cup onion, chopped
1 tablespoon olive oil
1½ cups vegetable broth
1 cup frozen green peas
⅓ cup spelt flour
1 roll refrigerated flaky biscuits
1 Worthington® vegetarian Dinner Roast, baked and cubed

Method

Cook carrots and potatoes with 1 cup of the water on low heat for 10 minutes; set aside.

Sauté mushrooms and onions in oil for 5 minutes in a large skillet.

Add broth, carrots, potatoes, and peas into skillet.

Wisk flour with the remaining ⅓ cup water in a small bowl until smooth, and stir into vegetable mixture.

Bring to boil over medium heat and stir to prevent lumps. Add diced dinner roast.

Open biscuit package and press half of it into glass 9x13-inch dish to form a crust.

Pour the mixture into pie crust and add remaining biscuits for the top crust.

Bake for 30–40 minutes at 350 degrees, or until filling is bubbly and crust is brown.

Chapter 5

Rice, Casseroles, and Sauces

Spiritizer

Your Insurance Policy

Devotional thought presented for the discussion topic on the Forum at GCE, "Insurance Policy."

Do you have an insurance policy? Is it for your home, your auto, your health, your life? You can get an insurance policy for just about anything these days, even your cat, your dog, or your bird. An insurance policy will eliminate, or at least minimize, your risks and liabilities.

> *Because of the INSURANCE policy Jesus executed on our behalf, we now have ASSURANCE—assurance of life everlasting.*

Terrestrial insurance is good but celestial insurance is far better. Jesus offers celestial insurance for all of us. However, He not only *offered* it, but He also paid a premium for it. And He paid the premium for us. Because of the INSURANCE policy Jesus executed on our behalf, we now have ASSURANCE—assurance of life everlasting.

In this world filled with the hurry and scurry of uneasiness and insecurity, God—through His Son—has provided the assurance of salvation. Be assured that this insurance is not based on our abilities, or capabilities, or our good works. This is something to be thankful for! On our own, we would never qualify for that priceless insurance.

"For by grace are ye saved through faith; and that not of yourselves: it is the gift of God: Not of works, lest any man should boast" (Eph. 2:8–9, KJV).

Thank you, Jesus, for Your *insurance*, and Your *assurance*.

As we walk our daily walk on this earth, may I implore you to think of God's INSURANCE and ASSURANCE policies every time you think of your terrestrial INSURANCE plan?

Lentils and Bulgur

1 pound cooked lentils
1 (13.5-ounce) can coconut milk
4 vegetarian chicken-style bouillon cubes, or 1 tablespoon seasonings of your choice
4 cups bulgur wheat, rinsed
1–2 tablespoons coconut oil (optional)
Boiling water

Method

Add coconut milk and bouillon cubes into 6-quart pot with cooked lentils and allow to dissolve. Add bulgur to pot and enough boiling water to bring liquid to reach no more than 2 inches above bulgur. Bring back up to boil, and then reduce heat to low so bulgur will cook slowly. If you have a rice cooker you may cook the bulgur in it on the white rice setting. After bulgur is cooked, add coconut oil and fluff with a fork to thoroughly mix in.

Note: You may adjust the ratio of lentils to bulgur to your liking.

Jamaican Rice and Peas

1 pound dried red kidney beans cooked in salted water until soft, but not mushy
4–5 cups short grain brown rice
2 (13.5 ounce) cans coconut milk
3–4 vegetarian bouillon cubes
1 teaspoon each of thyme, dried onion, and garlic powder
Hot water

Method

Wash rice and add to cook beans. Add coconut milk, bouillon cubes, and other seasonings. Add enough hot water to bring up to 2 inches above rice in an oven-safe, 8-quart pot. Bring to boil again and turn heat down to low for 45 minutes. Place pot in oven and cook rice at 350 degrees. Check rice after 45 minutes. Liquid should have been absorbed and rice soft but not soupy. If rice is not cooked, add a bit more hot water as necessary.

Mimi's Vegan Baked Macaroni Casserole

4 cups elbow macaroni
½ cup vegan margarine
½ cup flour
3½ cups boiling water
1 tablespoon salt
1 teaspoon sugar
Pinch of turmeric
1½ teaspoons garlic powder
1½ teaspoons onion powder
¼ cup coconut oil
¾ cup nutritional yeast

Method

Preheat oven at 350 degrees. Cook macaroni according to package, drain and set aside.

Melt margarine over low heat. Slowly whisk in the flour until bubbly. Whisk in boiling water, salt, sugar, turmeric, garlic powder, and onion powder. Once thick and bubbling, turn off heat and whisk in oil and nutritional yeast. Mix macaroni into sauce, place in a 9x11-inch baking dish, and bake for 30 minutes.

Savory Cashew Cream

2 cups raw cashews, soaked overnight
1 tablespoon fresh thyme leaves
2 teaspoons salt
¼ cup olive oil
Juice from ½ of a medium-sized lemon
Enough water to cover contents in blender

Method

Blend all ingredients in blender until smooth and creamy. Add more, or less, water depending on how thick or thin you want your cream.

Potato Casserole

2 pounds refrigerated shredded potato hash browns (Simply Potatoes® brand preferred)
1 can vegan cream of celery, or mushroom soup
2 cups shredded vegan cheddar cheese
½ cup onion, chopped
1 teaspoon salt
½ cup melted vegan margarine
2 cups vegan sour cream
¾ cup crushed corn flakes

Method

Place hash browns, cheese, salt, sour cream, and soup in a large bowl and mix together.
Sauté onion with margarine until translucent, about 3–5 minutes, then add to mixture in bowl. Pour mixture into a large glass baking dish. Sprinkle cornflakes on top.
Bake at 350 degrees for 45–60 minutes.
Note: "Vivian's brand" vegan cream soups can be found on Amazon.

Cheese Casserole

1 cup coconut milk, or plain soy milk
2 cups vegan cheddar cheese
1 pound firm tofu, coarsely chopped
1 cup wheat breadcrumbs
¼ cup margarine, melted
Salt and pepper to taste

Method

Place all ingredients together in a mixing bowl and mix thoroughly.

Pour into a 8x8-inch glass baking dish and bake for 30-60 minutes at 350 degrees until bubbly.

Broccoli Casserole

2 pounds chopped broccoli, cooked and drained
1 cup cooked bulgur wheat
1 cup cooked jasmine rice
2 cups shredded vegan cheddar cheese (more if you desire)
2 cans cream of mushroom or celery soup

Method

Mix all ingredients together and place in a 9x13-inch glass baking dish.

Bake at 350 degrees for 30 minutes or until top is brown.

Note: "Vivian's brand" vegan cream soups can be found on Amazon.

Chili Mac

1 (50-ounce) can Worthington® chili
1 (10.5-ounce) can cream of mushroom soup
2–3 cups vegan cheddar cheese
1 pound elbow macaroni, cooked and drained

Method

Place all the ingredients in a large bowl and mix together thoroughly.

Pour mixture into a large rectangular glass dish, and bake at 350 degrees for 30 minutes, or until slightly brown on top.

Note: "Vivian's brand" vegan cream soups can be found on Amazon.

Spiritizer

The Generation Gap

Devotional thought presented for the discussion topic on the Forum at GCE,

"The Generation Gap"

I had a prescription in front of me, and I had a problem; I could not read the name of the drug. The penmanship was terrible; the writing was illegible. Is this prescription for Tenex—an antihypertensive agent for high blood pressure, or is it for Xanax—an antianxiety agent that can be habit-forming and addictive?

I didn't know. I could not tell.

If I dispense Tenex and it should be Xanax, or vice versa, I would be misdispensing. I think in a way the youth and young adults of today believe that the older folks not only misdispense, but we misdiagnose, misprognose, and even mistreat their needs and concerns.

We dispense restriction when what they need instead is freedom.

We dispense constraint when what they need instead is space.

We dispense disapproval when what they need instead is approval.

We dispense lecture when what they need instead is example.

We dispense blame when what they need instead is praise … and the list goes on.

And by the way, that day when I got the illegible prescription I went ahead and dispensed the correct medication. How do I know that the right drug was dispensed? Well, prior to dispensing it, I picked up the phone and consulted with the prescriber.

I asked her for what medication did she write the prescription. I was told what it was, and I dispensed it. I dispensed the correct medicine by *communicating* with the prescriber. The operative word here is communication. I believe that by communicating with each other the older folks and the younger ones will be able to bridge this generation gap. It may not solve all the problems—but open communication is a good start.

Raspberry Sauce

2 tablespoons honey
2 tablespoons lemon juice
¼ cup low-sugar raspberry spread
2 tablespoons apple cider vinegar
2 cups fresh organic raspberries

Method

Blend well in blender and pour over salad, or use as a dipping sauce.

BBQ Sauce

1 large onion, chopped
2 tablespoons vegan margarine
1 cup ketchup
½ cup brown sugar
3 tablespoons lemon juice
3 tablespoons vegan Worcestershire sauce
2 tablespoons vinegar
½ teaspoon liquid smoke
1 teaspoon prepared mustard
1 teaspoon celery seed

Method

Sauté onions in margarine. Stir in all other ingredients and bring to a boil.

Lower heat and cook for 10 more minutes on low, stirring frequently.

Garlic Herb Sauce

¼ cup tahini
1 tablespoon fresh lemon juice
½ teaspoon fresh dill leaves
3 cloves garlic, grated
2–4 tablespoons nut milk, add a little at a time for a smooth consistency
Pinch of pink Himalayan salt

Method

Mix all ingredients well together and use as dip or sandwich spread.

Whole Cranberry Sauce

1 pound whole cranberries
1 cup fresh squeezed orange juice
½ cup water
¼ cup brown sugar
Pinch of salt

Method

Place all ingredients in a saucepan and cook over low heat until berries are soft and succulent.

Alfredo Sauce

- 12 ounces soft tofu
- ½ cup coconut milk
- 1 tablespoon coconut oil
- 2 tablespoons fresh basil, chopped
- 2 tablespoons nutritional yeast
- 3 cloves garlic, minced
- ½ teaspoon salt
- ½ teaspoon oregano
- ¼ teaspoon marjoram

Method

Blend all ingredients in a blender. Heat using a double boiler. Cook until thick but do not allow to boil.

Serve over cooked noodles.

Spinach Alfredo Sauce

- 1 pound frozen spinach, thawed and squeezed
- 1 pound soft tofu
- ½ cup plain soy milk

3 cloves garlic, crushed
2 tablespoons olive oil
4 tablespoons nutritional yeast
1 teaspoon sea salt
2 teaspoons onion powder
1 tablespoon organic peanut butter, optional

Method

Add all ingredients except for spinach into a blender or food processor and blend until creamy. Place cream mixture and spinach in a saucepan and slowly warm over low heat.

Pour over cooked and drained whole wheat pasta and serve.

Sweet and Sour Sauce 1

1 tablespoon ginger, peeled and chopped
3 stalks scallion
2 tablespoons oil
½ cup ketchup
1½ cups water
4 tablespoons brown sugar or molasses
2 tablespoons apple cider vinegar
1 tablespoon soy sauce
2 tablespoons cornstarch
1 teaspoon salt

Method

Stir fry ginger and scallion with oil. Add ketchup, water, sugar, vinegar, soy sauce, and salt and bring to a boil. Mix cornstarch with a little cold water and add to sauce.

Cook until it thickens.

Sweet and Sour Sauce 2

1 cup water
1 cup apple juice

- 5 tablespoons brown sugar
- 5 tablespoons apple cider vinegar
- 2 tablespoons cornstarch
- 2 tablespoons soy sauce
- 1 teaspoon salt

Method

Combine all ingredients in a saucepan and let simmer until thick.

Lemon Cashew Sauce

- 1½ cups raw cashews, soaked overnight
- 2 cloves garlic
- 2 teaspoons ground coriander
- ½ tablespoon mustard seed
- 4 tablespoons fresh lemon juice
- ½ cup warm water
- ¼ teaspoon vegetarian chicken-style seasoning or plain salt

Method

Place all ingredients in a blender and blend until creamy.

Tomatoes and Peanut Sauce

- 1 cup raw or roasted peanuts
- 2 large tomatoes, washed and chopped
- ½ cup onions, chopped
- 4 large carrots, cut in pieces
- 2 tablespoons peanut or palm oil
- Seasonings of choice
- Salt

Method

Grind peanuts until smooth in mortar or food processor.

Sauté tomatoes, carrots, onions, and seasonings with oil until cooked—add a little water if needed.

Add ground peanuts and let simmer for 5–10 minutes.

Tomato Sauce

- 1 large onion, chopped
- 4 cloves garlic, chopped
- 3 tablespoons olive oil
- 2 large tomatoes, diced
- 2 tablespoons vegan Worcestershire sauce
- 2 tablespoons apple cider vinegar

Method

Sauté onions and garlic in olive oil. Add tomatoes, Worcestershire sauce, and apple cider vinegar and let simmer until thick.

Let cool then puree with blender. Serve that day with oven fries or baked potato.

Ginger Sauce

- ½ cup onion, chopped
- 2 cups red bell peppers, chopped
- 2 cloves garlic, minced
- 4 teaspoons olive oil
- ½ cup pineapple juice
- ½ cup apple jelly
- 4 teaspoons fresh grated ginger

Method

Sauté onions, peppers, and garlic in the olive oil until onions are translucent. Add the pineapple juice, apple jelly, and ginger and allow to simmer for 15–20 minutes.

White Sauce

5 tablespoons vegan butter
¼ cup flour
2 teaspoons salt
¼ teaspoon nutmeg
1 quart coconut milk
1–2 cups white vegan cheddar cheese

Method

Make a roux with butter and flour by melting the butter over medium heat in a large saucepan and then blending in the flour and cooking for a minute or two until the flour no longer smells raw. Add the other ingredients and whisk well. Bring to a boil, stirring constantly, lower heat and simmer until thick. Do not allow to burn.

Note: You may also use unsweetened soy milk for this recipe, but coconut milk works best.

Meatballs and Sauce

1 cup water
1½ cups ketchup
1 tablespoon apple cider vinegar
½ cup brown sugar
2 teaspoons garlic, chopped
1 cup onion, chopped
3 tablespoons vegan Worcester sauce
1 pound vegetarian meat balls of choice

Method

Mix all ingredients and pour over meat balls. Cover and bake for 30-45 minutes at 350 degrees.

Rice, Casseroles, and Sauces ◆ 125

Dipping Sauce and Dressing

1 cup water
½ cup raw cashews, soaked overnight
½ cup lemon juice
½ cup coconut oil
2 cloves garlic
2 tablespoons honey
1½ teaspoons salt
1½ teaspoons onion powder
1 teaspoon dill

Method

Combine all ingredients except for dill in a blender and blend until smooth. Whisk in dill.

Great for dipping fresh vegetable spears or drizzling over salads.

Note: This is enough sauce to last for a week of fresh vegetable salads.

Basic Tomato Peanut Butter Sauce

1 medium onion, diced
1 cup tomato paste
1 cup peanut butter
1 cup water
1 clove garlic, crushed
Salt and pepper to taste
1 tablespoon oil

Method

Sauté onion with oil until translucent and add all other ingredients. Simmer slowly so sauce will not burn.

You may add firm tofu cubes, gluten pieces, or your favorite vegetarian meat into simmering pot.

Peanut and Tomato Sauce

1 tablespoon tomato paste
¼ cup organic peanut butter
1 cup coconut milk
½ teaspoon onion powder
½ teaspoon garlic powder
¼ teaspoon fresh black pepper
½ teaspoon sea salt

Method

Place all ingredients into a saucepan and simmer over low heat for 10–15 minutes. This sauce may be used to simmer tofu cubes or gluten pieces. You can even pour it over some cooked brown rice or bulgur.

Chapter 6

Sandwiches, Spreads, and Pestos

Spiritizer
Shyness

Devotional thought presented for the discussion topic on the Forum at GCE, "Shyness."

If you are reserved, or if you show nervousness and timidity in the company of others, then you are shy. Other words that define shyness are bashful, sheepish, and introverted. There is another word that defines shyness as well; it is diffidence—or lack of self-confidence. Not all introverts or shy people lack self-confidence, but it is a common trait. I think that one describes me when I was growing up. I was never self-confident growing up.

Perhaps that's because I was repeatedly told by my dad and others (sometimes unmaliciously) that I was either acting feminine, or I was too soft. I was often told to be quiet, and not speak, or that I was just simply called dunce.

In the end my father was proud of me because ultimately, I was the only one on either side of the family (a total of twenty-two—twelve from my mother's side and ten from father's) who defied the odds and attended high school, college, and university. Now, this was not because of any sudden dose of brilliance, ingenuity, cognition, precocity or any such thing. No. God was just good to me because He knew my heart. So it was not good luck but God's fortune. I remember attending primary school barefooted up to the 8th grade. I probably did in the 9th grade too, but I can't remember. Now there were other children attending school barefooted, but it was a small minority.

I was so conscious of my rustic lifestyle that I stayed away from students that looked better off and behaved better than I. When I became an Adventist, things began to change. The young people in my church all clung together. We sang together, worshipped together, stuck together. We even competed with—and sometimes against—each other. We were a family.

Then I went to college and came across a group of Adventist students in a fraternity called Advent Fellowship. And what a fellowship that was! We were a real family—like real brothers and sisters. That did so much to boost my self-esteem. As a matter of fact a lot of us reunited in November of 2019 on the occasion of the 50th Anniversary of Advent Fellowship on the campus of the University of the West Indies (UWI) in Jamaica. What a time it was—brothers and sisters in the Lord hugging and reminiscing.[1]

> *The way you overcome shyness is to become so wrapped up in something that you forget to be afraid.*

Claudia Lady Bird Johnson said that the way you overcome shyness is to become so wrapped up in something that you forget to be afraid. I did that at my small Adventist church in Morant Bay Jamaica. I did that on a larger scale at college among my Adventist colleagues, and I am doing this now with my family, my church, and GCE.

So are you shy? That's OK. Kirkpatrick Sale says it perfectly:

> Everyone is shy—it is the inborn modesty that makes us able to live in harmony with other creatures and our fellows. Achievement comes not by denying shyness but, occasionally, by setting it aside and letting pride and perspiration come first.

You should not stay in a state of shyness. That does not mean you have to change your colors if you are an introvert, however. You may never want to be the center of a party or the rousing leader. But you can overcome the behavior of shyness and act with confidence in whatever role God gives you in your life. Moses came out of shyness with God's grace to be one of the greatest leaders of the Bible because God gave him a role bigger than himself. So, act confidently, be engaged in something outside of yourself, try new things, take on new tasks—especially the ones you are afraid of. Talk, do presentations, make yourself vulnerable sometimes. Practice and go for it.

> *"For God has not given us the spirit of fear, but of power and of love and of a sound mind."*
> *(2 Timothy 1:7)*

---

1 I wrote the theme song for this group and they are still singing it today—forty-four years later. You can watch and listen at the following links: **https://1ref.us/239**, **https://1ref.us/23a**, and **https://1ref.us/23b**.

Cream Cheese and Raisin Sandwich

1 package soft vegan cream cheese
1 cup carrots, shredded
¾ cup raisins
2 tablespoons vegan mayonnaise

Method

Pulse chop all items with a food processor and spread over bread.
Note: Refrigeration will make product hard to spread.

Mock Egg Salad Sandwich

⅓ cup red bell peppers, diced
⅓ cup carrots, shredded
2 stalks celery, finely chopped
2 cups extra firm tofu, finely chopped with a pastry cutter
4 tablespoons vegan mayonnaise
1 teaspoon lemon juice
2 tablespoons slivered almonds
Pinch of turmeric
Salt and pepper to taste

Method

Place peppers, carrots, and celery into a large mixing bowl.
Gently fold in tofu, mayonnaise, lemon juice, almonds, turmeric, salt, and pepper.
Refrigerate overnight.

Mock Tuna Salad

1 (15.5-ounce) can garbanzo beans, drained and rinsed
¼ cup vegan mayonnaise
1–2 sheets seaweed (nori), chopped
5–10 capers, chopped
1 tablespoon fresh lemon juice
1 tablespoon soy sauce

1 tablespoon nutritional yeast
½ teaspoon garlic powder
½ tablespoon prepared mustard
½ teaspoon white vinegar
Sea salt and black pepper to taste.

Method

Mash garbanzo beans coarsely with a fork. Add all other ingredients and mix together well.

Allow to sit for at least 30 minutes so flavors will blend. Serve with multigrain bread or lettuce leaves.

Game Night Sandwich

1 loaf wheat or multi-grain Italian bread
2 tablespoons vegan mayonnaise
2 tablespoons soft vegan margarine
1 tablespoon prepared mustard
1 tablespoon dried parsley
1 tablespoon dried oregano
2 firm ripe red or yellow tomatoes, sliced
Slices of red and orange bell peppers
Slices of vegan provolone or mozzarella cheese
8 ounces vegetarian deli turkey slices
8 ounces vegetarian deli salami slices
Baby spinach leaves

Method

Slice bread across in ½ inch slices, leaving slices attached at the bottom.

Combine mayonnaise, margarine, mustard, parsley and oregano and spread evenly on every other slice of the bread.

Next, add the tomatoes, peppers, cheese, and deli slices alternatively between the bread slices.

Wrap in foil paper and place in oven at 350 degrees for 20–30 minutes.

Remove from oven and separate the sandwiches.

Mock Chicken Salad

2 cups vegetarian chicken, cubed
1 cup vegan mayonnaise
½ cup celery, diced
½ cup green grapes, sliced in quarters
½ cup pecan pieces
½ cup garbanzo beans, roughly mashed
1 teaspoon chicken style seasoning
Pinch of turmeric

Method

Place all ingredients into large bowl and mix well. You may substitute sweet cranberries instead of grapes. Use to fill pita bread or tortilla wraps.

Mushroom Sandwich

5 cups portabella mushrooms, sliced
½ cup fresh tomatoes, diced
1 large red onion, sliced
½ jalapeño pepper, sliced, optional
1 large green bell pepper, sliced
3 cloves garlic, minced
6 tablespoons vegan margarine
4 tablespoons nutritional yeast
1–2 packets beef-style George Washington broth
Fresh basil leaves, chopped

Method

Heat skillet and sauté mushrooms, tomatoes, onions, peppers, and garlic with margarine.

Add nutritional yeast and broth packets. Allow to cook on low heat for 15–20 minutes uncovered. Spoon onto warm multi-grain sandwich bread and top with chopped fresh basil.

Hot Bean Sandwich

1 medium onion, chopped
1 clove garlic, minced
1 medium jalapeño, chopped
¼ cup red bell pepper, chopped
¼ cup green bell pepper, chopped
1 tablespoon coconut oil
½ cup textured vegetable protein (TVP), soaked and drained
2 tablespoons nutritional yeast
1 tablespoon vegetarian beef-style seasoning
1 can vegetarian baked beans
4 multi-grain hamburger buns

Method

Sauté onion, garlic, and peppers with coconut oil in a skillet.
Add textured vegetable protein, nutritional yeast, and seasoning.
Allow to simmer for 3 minutes.
Add baked beans and allow to simmer for 10 more minutes.
Cut hamburger buns open and spoon in bean filling to make a hot sandwich.

Crazy Hoagie

1 tablespoon organic peanut butter
1 multigrain hoagie roll
4 slices ripe avocado
2 slices smoked tofu
3 slices firm ripe tomatoes
5–6 fresh spinach leaves
Drizzle of zesty Italian dressing

Method

Spread peanut butter on bread slices.

Layer with slices of avocado, tofu, tomatoes, and spinach leaves.

Drizzle dressing over sandwich filling and make sandwich.

Mock Chicken/Turkey Sandwich

4 ounces vegetarian chicken deli slices
4 ounces vegetarian turkey deli slices
¼ cup pickle relish
1 small red onion, minced, optional
½ cup vegan mayonnaise
⅛ teaspoon celery seeds
Lettuce leaves
Sliced tomatoes
Multigrain bread

Method

Place deli slices, relish, onion, mayonnaise, and celery seeds into a food processor. Pulse a few times for a coarse chop. Spread on bread and serve with lettuce leaves and sliced tomatoes.

Simple Sandwich

2 slices multi-grain bread, lightly toasted and buttered
2 tablespoons hummus spread
¼ cup carrot, shredded
Baby spinach leaves
1 tablespoon raisins

Method

Spread hummus over each slice of bread. Layer with carrots and spinach.

Sprinkle raisins on top to complete one sandwich.

Pita Pocket Sandwiches

1 package whole wheat pita bread
1 (15-ounce) can black beans, rinsed and drained
1 (15-ounce) can sweet corn, drained

1 cup red bell pepper, chopped
1 cup green bell pepper, chopped
2 firm ripe avocados, diced
2 cups seedless cucumbers, chopped
2 cups fresh spinach, chopped
2 tablespoons nutritional yeast
½ cup vegan mayonnaise, or dressing of choice

Method

Place all ingredients into a large bowl and toss together lightly. Fill pita pockets with filling.

Party Wrap

2 (30-ounce) cans black beans, rinsed and drained
1 (15.5-ounce) can kidney beans, rinsed and drained
3 cups bulgur wheat or quinoa, cooked and cooled
2 cups shredded vegan cheddar cheese
2 cups romaine lettuce, shredded
2 cups red cabbage, shredded
3 ripe avocados, diced
2 cups firm ripe tomatoes, diced
Vegan ranch dressing
10 whole wheat or vegetable tortilla wraps, kept warm

Method

Place beans, bulgur, and cheese into a large bowl and mix together.

In a separate bowl, toss lettuce, cabbage, avocado, and tomatoes with dressing.

Place one warm tortilla on counter and put heaps of bean, bulgur, and cheese mixture in center.

Next, add the salad mix on top and roll up like a burrito.

Cut each wrap in two halves and secure each half with a toothpick.

Submarine Sandwich Filling

1 tablespoon extra-virgin olive oil
¼ cup onion, sliced
2 cloves garlic, minced
1 cup tomatoes, chopped
¼ cup green bell pepper, sliced
¼ cup red bell pepper, sliced
1 cup portabella mushrooms, sliced
2 tablespoons soy sauce
1 tablespoon nutritional yeast

Method

Heat oil in skillet on medium heat. Sauté the onions, garlic, tomatoes, peppers, and mushrooms until soft—about 6–8 minutes.

Add soy sauce and nutritional yeast and incorporate well.

Cover skillet and let simmer for 5 minutes over low heat.

Serving suggestion: This may be served on a toasted submarine (hoagie) roll.

Carrot and Nut Sandwich

½ cup carrots, shredded
¼ cup green bell pepper, thinly sliced
½ teaspoon lime juice
2 tablespoons mayonnaise
¼ cup chopped salted nuts or seeds of choice
2 slices wheat bread

Method

Place carrots, peppers, and lime juice in a mixing bowl and mix thoroughly.

Add mayonnaise and mix again. Spread on sandwich bread and then sprinkle minced nuts on top.

Be aware of nut allergies when choosing nuts and seeds.

PB, Carrots, and Raisin Sandwich

2 tablespoons smooth soft organic peanut butter
2 medium carrots, grated
¼ cup raisins, chopped
¼ cup mayonnaise
1 large whole wheat tortilla wrap, warmed

Method

Place all items except tortilla wrap together in a bowl and mix thoroughly.

Put mixture in center of wrap and fold up like a burrito.

Ripe Plantain Sandwich

6 pieces ripe plantain, fried
2 slices ripe tomatoes
2 strips vegetarian bacon, cooked
Lettuce leaves
2 slices multigrain bread spread with vegan mayonnaise

Method

Arrange all items on sandwich bread and enjoy.

Spiritizer

Grieving

Devotional thought presented for the discussion topic on the Forum at GCE, "Grieving."

Recently a pastor friend made us aware of the concerns he had for a dear member of his congregation whose husband was ill and hospitalized. A Few days later he got the sad news that he died.

We grieved and mourned as my pastor friend's brother told us about a dear church sister and friend who he spoke with at length one evening, only to receive a call early the next morning—only a few hours later—that there had been a tragic accident! The sister was struck by a vehicle and died.

And we grieved and mourned.

There was one year at our church in Maryland when we wondered how much more we could bear. First, a beautiful, wonderful, well-loved teenager had a brain aneurism and died. Before we knew she passed we heard that she was rushed to the hospital. She was a very close friend of my daughter. As my daughter cried, I prayed with her and, trying to console her, I told her that her friend would not die. But she did. In fact, she was already dead, but we did not know it then. And in my daughter's anguish she cried and said, "But Dad, you promised she would not die." I was speechless.

And we grieved and mourned.

Then a dear church brother of ours who worked as maintenance personnel at a nearby airport was in one of the plane's engines cleaning it. The pilot, who was unaware that he was there, started the ignition. The engine roared to life, and our church brother was no longer.

And we grieved and mourned.

Following that, an older couple who had just buried their mother/mother-in-law earlier in the day was driving home that night when their car was struck by a drunk driver and both perished.

And we grieved and mourned.

We have all been touched one way or another by the agonizing grief and pain caused by the loss of a family member, or dear friend, or a friend of a friend, or even people we do not know personally but may just have admiration for.

In the parable of the wheat and the tares in Matthew 13:24–30 the servant asks the master, "Who did this? Who sowed the tares among the wheat?"

The master answered: "An enemy has done this" (Matt. 13:28).

Friends, don't ever forget this: An enemy has done this. He has been doing this; he is doing this, and will continue to do this, until the second coming of our Lord and Savior.

In times like these you will feel the anguish, and the pain, and the grief—sometimes you will even cry out, "WHO DID THIS?" Remember, an enemy did it. But hold on; a Friend will undo it and make it right again some day. What a FRIEND we have in Jesus!

- Can you hear Jesus on the cross? "Eloi, Eloi, Lama Sabachthani" (Mark 15:34). I know how it translates, but to me it is:

- "My God, My God, who did this?"

- Yes, my friends, an enemy has done this, but the good news is we have a High Priest who can empathize and sympathize with the feelings of our infirmities (Heb. 4:15) and our grief.

- Please note that in times like these there are coping mechanisms we can incorporate and employ in our lives, to help us not grieve as those without hope (see 1 Thess. 4:13).

- And one of those mechanisms is leaning on the promises of a resurrection of eternal life in the future. Because "then shall be brought to pass the saying that is written, Death is swallowed up in victory. O death, where is they sting? O grave, where is they victory?" (1 Cor. 15:54–55, KJV).

Garbanzo Spread

2 cups cooked garbanzo beans
2 tablespoons olive oil
1 tablespoon tomato paste
2 tablespoons nutritional yeast
2 tablespoons vegan mayonnaise
1 teaspoon chopped red onion, chopped, optional

Method

Place garbanzos into a mixing bowl and mash with fork. Mix in other ingredients with fork and blend well.

Note: While a food processor would give a much smoother texture, using a fork will save you the time of cleaning up your food processor. Use as a spread for your favorite sandwich or with crackers. You may also cut plum tomatoes in half, scoop out seeds, then fill with spread for an appetizer.

Party Spread

1 pound extra firm tofu, drained
8 ounces vegetarian ham deli slices, thawed
8 ounces vegetarian chicken deli slices, thawed
½ cup vegan mayonnaise
1 small red onion, minced, optional
1 block vegan cream cheese at room temperature
½ cup walnuts or almonds, toasted and chopped
1 tablespoon ketchup
1 tablespoon nutritional yeast
Salt and pepper (optional)
¼ cup carrots, shredded

Method

Place all items into food processor (except carrots) and pulse until ingredients are coarsely chopped and combined. Scrape mixture into a bowl and mix in carrots.

Serve on crackers or bread.

Avocado Spread

1 can green peas, drained and coarsely mashed
2 firm ripe avocados, coarsely mashed
1–2 teaspoons fresh lime juice
Dash of Spike® seasoning

Method

Mix all ingredients and spread on whole wheat bread with sliced tomatoes and lettuce.

Not-Ham Sandwich Spread

2 cups vegetarian ham, grated, from frozen roll (by Worthington® meatless ham or Wham®, found in Adventist health food stores)
1 cup vegan cream cheese, at room temperature
¼ cup vegan mayonnaise, more if desired
¼ cup ketchup
1 small red onion, minced or grated, optional

Method

Shred frozen meatless ham roll on a 4-sided grater. Blend grated ham, cream cheese, mayonnaise, ketchup, and onions together with a sturdy spoon.

Let mixture sit for a few minutes on countertop so it will be easier to spread.

Blueberry Chia Spread

2½ cups fresh blueberries
1–2 tablespoons maple syrup
1 vanilla bean, scraped
2 tablespoons chia seeds
¼ cup water

Method

Combine berries, syrup, scraped vanilla bean seeds, and pod into a pot and simmer on low heat until berries burst and mixture is juicy. Add chia seeds and turn off heat. Remove bean pod, mix well, and place in refrigerator overnight.

Easy Guacamole

1 large ripe avocado, chopped
1 medium firm ripe tomato, seeded, chopped, and drained
1 small red onion, minced, optional
1 tablespoon lime juice
½ teaspoon salt
¼ teaspoon pepper
½ cup fennel, chopped

Method

Place everything into a plastic zipper bag and squeeze gently with both hands.
Squeeze out into a dish and toss the bag (one less container to wash).
Use as a dip or sandwich spread.

Tofu Vegan Mayo

2 cups soft tofu
1 tablespoon liquid lecithin
Juice from 1 lemon
¼ cup red bell pepper, seeded
1 tablespoon zesty Italian dressing

1 teaspoon Spike®
1 teaspoon garlic powder
1 teaspoon onion powder
1 teaspoon smoked paprika
Pinch of sage
Pinch of saffron

Method

Place all ingredients in a blender and blend until smooth. Store in refrigerator. Use within 7 days.

Cashew Vegan Mayo

1 cup raw cashews, soaked overnight
3 pitted dates
Juice from 1 large lemon
5–6 tablespoons water
½ teaspoon salt
1 teaspoon chopped jalapeño pepper

Method

Place all ingredients in blender and blend until smooth and creamy. Store in refrigerator. Use within 7 days.

Red Pepper Pâté

2 cups red bell pepper, diced
1 cup walnuts
3 large cloves garlic
Dash cayenne pepper
2 tablespoons olive oil

Method

Place pepper, walnuts, garlic, and cayenne in food processor or blender. Process until smooth.
While processor is still running, slowly pour in oil.
Pour mixture into a mold and refrigerate overnight.
Un-mold and serve with crackers or veggies.
Serving Suggestion: This can also be used as a sandwich spread.

Basil Pesto 1

1 bunch fresh basil
1 cup raw cashews (you may substitute walnuts, almonds, or macadamia nut pieces)
5 cloves garlic
1 cup nutritional yeast
2 teaspoons vegetarian chicken-style seasoning
Salt and pepper to taste
1 jalapeño, optional
½ cup olive oil

Method

Place basil, nuts, garlic, nutritional yeast, chicken-style seasoning, salt, pepper, and jalapeño (if desired) into a food processor and pulse for 30 seconds.

Slowly add the oil into the processor and pulse for another 30 seconds or until desired consistency.

Serving Suggestion: This can be poured over oven baked potatoes, cooked pasta, spread on bread for sandwiches, or used as a dressing for any salad.

Basil Pesto 2

1 cup fresh basil
½ cup fresh spinach
½ cup fresh parsley
8 cloves garlic
½ cup raw almonds, soaked overnight
½ of a medium jalapeño pepper
1 cup nutritional yeast
1 tablespoon vegetarian chicken-style seasoning, more if desired
Salt to taste
½ cup olive oil

Method

Place all ingredients into a food processor except olive oil, and pulse until blended well. While processor is still running, slowly drizzle olive oil over mixture. Do not completely puree pesto; allow for some chunks for better texture.

Black Pesto

1 cup black olives, washed and drained
½ cup nutritional yeast
2–3 tablespoons olive oil
1 teaspoon garlic, minced
½ cup fresh basil leaves
1 teaspoon vegetarian beef-style seasoning, more if desired

Method

Place all ingredients in a food processor and blend to desired consistency.

Walnut Pesto

1 cup walnuts
½ cup nutritional yeast
¼ cup fresh parsley
½ cup fresh basil
¼ cup olive oil
1–2 teaspoons vegetarian chicken-style seasoning

Method

Pulse all the ingredients in a food processor and process until smooth.

Pesto Sauce for Root Vegetables

¼ cup raw sunflower seeds
5 cloves garlic
3 sprigs fresh dill weed
3 tablespoons olive oil
1 large onion, chopped
½ bunch fresh parsley
2 cups fresh spinach
1 bunch fresh basil
1–2 vegetarian bouillon cubes
1 cup vegan sour cream
¼ cup nutritional yeast
1–2 cups soy milk

Method

Place all ingredients in a blender and puree until smooth. Pour contents over cooked hot root vegetables, such as cassava, yams. or potatoes.
Serving Suggestion: This pesto may also be poured over cooked pasta.

Three Bean Spread

1 (15-ounce) can garbanzo beans, washed and drained
1 (15-ounce) can kidney beans, washed and drained
1 (15-ounce) can pinto beans, washed and drained
Juice from 1 large lemon
Salt to taste
4 tablespoons olive oil
1 sprig green onions, chopped
1 small red onion, chopped, optional
¼ teaspoon fresh thyme leaves

Method

Place beans in a large bowl with lemon juice and salt, then coarsely mash with a potato masher or fork.
Pour out beans onto a platter and drizzle with olive oil.
Garnish with green and red onions and thyme leaves.
Cover and chill for 30 minutes.
Serving Suggestion: Serve with warm pita bread, crusty multi-grain bread, or crackers.

Sunflower and Sesame Seed Spread

½–1 cup pan-roasted sunflower seeds
½ cup raw sesame seeds
About ¼ cup extra virgin olive oil

Method

Place seeds in a food processor and whiz while adding oil very slowly.
Process for 3–5 minutes, or until smooth.
Serving Suggestion: Use like peanut butter.

Spiritizer
Spiritual Antidepressants

If you were to visit your doctor and were diagnosed for the first time with a condition such as diabetes, hyperlipidemia, hypertension, HIV/AIDS, or for sure, cancer, it is more than likely that your doctor would write you a prescription for an antidepressant—along with the other appropriate medication(s) for the condition(s) diagnosed. The reason for this is that you would surely be depressed after a diagnosis of any of the above medical conditions.

Over 15 million Americans are on antidepressants. It's the third most frequently prescribed category of medicine in the United States.

As a matter of fact, antidepressants are now even being prescribed for unlabeled uses such as drug abuse and dependency, attention deficit hyperactivity disorder (ADHD) both in children and adults, autism, eating disorders, fibromyalgia, premenstrual dysphoria disorder, and more.

I used to believe that depression was one of those medical conditions concocted by doctors and the pharmaceutical companies in order to fleece the people out of money.

I have not totally discarded this belief, but I now have a different perspective on depression ever since I read this quotation in the book *Ministry of Healing*, page 241. (Please pay attention to the words chosen because we don't write, or talk, like this anymore, and they are powerful):

> The **relation** that exists between the **mind** and the **body** is very **intimate**. When one is **affected**, the other **sympathizes**. **The condition of the mind affects the health to a far greater degree than many realize. Many of the diseases from which men suffer are the result of mental depression. Grief, anxiety, discontent, remorse, guilt, distrust,** all tend to **break down the life forces** and to **invite decay and death**. (emphasis supplied)

The quotation says it all. Depression is real. It can be triggered by one or a combination of emotions, and it can destroy not just the mind, but the whole body and soul. Is there a treatment or antidote for these deadly stressors that can lead to depression and despondency? Ellen White continues: "Courage, hope, faith, sympathy, love, promote health and prolong life" (ibid.).

> *There is a mindset that is indispensable to good health and optimum sanity—courage, hope, faith, sympathy, and love.*

What a novel concept! So, you thought the answer lies in medications, or even diet, exercise, and lifestyle changes? Ah, those are important, but there is a mindset that is indispensable to good health and optimum sanity—courage, hope, faith, sympathy, and love.

It might sound simple and unscientific, but try it—it might just work.

Avoid, if you can, man-made antidepressants and anti-anxiety agents and high-dose yourself on heaven's mental medicines—courage, hope, faith, sympathy, love, and the staying power of Jesus.

A contented mind, a cheerful spirit, is health to the body and strength to the soul. "A merry [rejoicing] heart doeth good like a medicine" (Prov. 17:22, KJV).

Chapter 7

Desserts, Breads, and Rolls

Spiritizer

The Suture Story

I had a cosmetic surgery a couple months ago.

A cyst or abnormal sac was growing underneath the skin on the left side of my face. It was a subtle, insidious growth. It was there, just dormant. It was unnoticeable at first. I knew it was there, but it didn't bother me at all, and no one noticed it—I don't think.

Then suddenly it started growing and becoming a large lump under my skin. Each time I looked in the mirror I noticed that my face was becoming increasingly misproportioned. The sides of my face were becoming uneven, and now people were beginning to notice.

My wife said: "Dear, I think it's time for you to take care of that growth on your face."

This kind of remined me of the SIN problem. It started in the heart, mind, and thinking of this magnificent being in heaven called Lucifer. His pride, ambition, and insurrection plan were not obvious to the others at the beginning. It was deceitfully artful, crafty, and cunning, until suddenly one third of the angels in heaven (thousands of them) were duped into his scheme, and the problem had to be addressed. Lucifer and his cohorts were evicted.

Perhaps the remaining angels, and the beings of the other worlds, did not realize or understand the subtle, devious nature of Satan's plan until he cunningly tricked Eve into sinning by disobeying God.

I sat on the operating chair in the surgeon's office, and she said that the time was come to deal with the growth on my face. The time was come for her to operate on it. Galatians 4:4 informs us that when the fullness of time was come God sent His Son, Jesus, to redeem us from the SIN problem.

It took about two years for the growth on my face to get to the point where I decided that it was time to remove it. It took over four thousand years for God to send His Son, Jesus, to operate on the SIN problem, but it happened at the right and appropriate time. The SIN problem was growing out of hand, and it was time for God to operate on it. "But when the fullness of the time was come, God sent forth his Son, made of a woman, made under the law, to redeem them that were under the law, that we might receive the adoption of sons" (Gal. 4:4, AKJV).

Sitting in the operating chair in the surgeon's office I watched and observed her with anxious anticipation as she worked on my face. She swabbed it with alcohol to remove dirt and germs. She applied a local anesthetic to deaden the pain of the needle she was about to pierce my skin with, in order to inject more of the anesthetic so that I would not feel the sharpness of the scalpel she was about to use to cut my skin.

Jesus came to remove not just the unsightly, but deadly lump of SIN from our body. If you want to observe the best surgeon at work, read about Him in the Gospels. Though He was God, He grew up being obedient to His parents. The Bible puts it this way: "Jesus grew in wisdom and in stature and in favor with God and all the people" (Luke 2:52, NLT).

> Read about it and observe the Master Surgeon at work as He operated on the SIN problem. And He is still doing it now:
> He supplies mercy to the struggling soul.
> He sustains the tempted and the tried.
> He sympathizes with the wounded and the broken.
> He strengthens the weak and the weary.
> He guards and he guides the wanderer.
> He heals the sick and cleanses the leper.
> He delivers the captives and defends the helpless,
> And binds up the broken-hearted. (*God For US. You Can Trust Him*, Don Moen, p. 158)

As the surgeon worked on my face, I observed her well. I felt the movements. I felt the pressure exerted on my face. I felt the maneuvers as she slowly, but deliberately, incised away the unwanted, unsightly lump under my skin. But there was no pain. The anesthesia camouflaged and absorbed the pain for me. That's what Jesus did for us:

Isaiah 53:5 (NIV) tells us: "But he was pierced for our transgressions, he was crushed for our iniquities; the punishment that brought us peace was on him, and by his wounds we are healed."

Ellen White puts it this way in *The Desire of Ages* (p. 25):

Christ was treated as we deserve that we may be treated as He deserves. He was condemned for our sins, in which He had no share, that we might be justified by His righteousness, in which we had no share. He suffered the death, which was ours, that we might receive the life which was His. By His stripes we are healed.

When the surgeon was finished, her assistants sutured up the incision on my face, sent me home to heal, and said: "Return in seven days so that we can remove the stitches to facilitate permanent healing."

Jesus finished His surgery on sin on the cross. He sutured the wounds. Now we are in the healing process as He ministers to the Father as our High Priest in heaven.

But we still have the incision and suture of sin on us. But He will return to remove the sutures and bring about final healing and restoration to the SIN LUMP, the SIN CYST, problem.

I did not look forward to returning to the doctor's office to remove the sutures because I did not know if I would feel any pain, and I am petrified of pain. I can tell you now that the procedure was not painful. In fact, I was surprised when she said the procedure was over.

I am looking forward for that glorious day when Jesus returns to remove the sutures from His incision of the sin surgery. And He promised: no more pain, no more crying, no more sickness, or death. And more importantly, NO MORE SIN. So friends, Jesus has already performed the surgery on sin. Relax, obey His instructions, and let it heal.

My surgeon's instructions to me before the removal of the sutures were: "Remove the bandage and tape in 24 hours. Apply a small amount of the antibiotic ointment I have prescribed for you. Cover it with a broad Band-Aid®. Do this every twenty-four hours and return in seven days for suture removal.

I think I hear Jesus saying to you and me: "I performed the surgery successfully. If you love Me, keep my commandments. They are not grievous. My sheep know my voice and they follow me. Loose the bands of wickedness, undo the heavy burdens, let the oppressed go free, break every yoke. Deal thy bread to the hungry, give shelter to the poor. Clothe the naked and take care of your family" (John 4:15, 1 John 5:3, Isa. 58:6, 7, paraphrased by me).

So, let's purpose in our hearts to follow the Great Surgeon's instruction so that we can gladly make our appointment on that great suture removal day. "Even so Lord, Jesus. Come quickly" (Rev. 22:20, paraphrased).

Banana Bran Muffin

Dry ingredients:
1 cup all-purpose flour
1 cup wheat bran
1 tablespoon cornstarch
3 teaspoons baking powder
¼ teaspoon salt
¼ cup brown sugar

Wet ingredients:
2 ripe bananas, mashed
⅔ cup soy milk
2 tablespoons melted margarine
½ cup prunes, chopped

Method

Combine all dry ingredients into one bowl and mix well. In another bowl combine the wet ingredients.

Add the wet ingredients to the dry ingredients and mix well. Turn out into well-greased muffin tins.

Bake for 25–30 minutes at 350 degrees.

Makes 4–6 muffins.

Banana Bread 1

2 large bananas, sliced
½ cup brown sugar
½ cup oil
¼ cup Craisins®
¼ teaspoon cinnamon
Dash of salt
⅛ teaspoon nutmeg
1 teaspoon vanilla
1½ cups whole wheat flour
1½ teaspoons baking powder
½ teaspoon baking soda

Method

Puree banana with sugar in a blender. Pour into a bowl, and add oil, Craisins®, cinnamon, salt, nutmeg, and vanilla, and mix well. Sieve the flour, baking powder, and baking soda directly into pureed mixture. Gently fold into wet ingredients (do not stir). Pour into greased loaf pan and bake in preheated oven at 350 degrees for 40–60 minutes.

Banana Bread 2

2 tablespoons ground flaxseeds
6 tablespoons warm water
6 ripe bananas, mashed
1 stick vegan margarine, melted
1½ cups brown sugar
1 teaspoon vanilla
3 cups sifted whole wheat flour
2 teaspoons baking soda

Method

Mix ground flaxseeds with water and set aside for 10 minutes. After the flaxseeds have rested for 10 minutes, mix together mashed bananas, melted margarine, flaxseed mixture, sugar, and vanilla.

Add the flour and baking soda. Mix well but do not overmix.
Place in greased loaf pan.
Bake in a 350-degree preheated oven for 45–60 minutes. Cool before slicing.

Carrot Cake/Muffins

1¼ cups sugar
1 cup oil
2 cups all-purpose flour
4 tablespoons corn starch
2 teaspoons baking soda
2 teaspoons cinnamon
1 teaspoon salt
2 cups carrots, shredded
1 (8-ounce) can crushed pineapple with juice
¼ cup chopped walnuts, optional
1 cup raisins, optional
2 cups apples, shredded, optional
1 cup fresh grated coconut, optional

Method

Preheat oven at 350 degrees. Grease and flour a round cake pan or muffin tins.
Beat sugar and oil until well blended–about two minutes with a hand mixer.

In a bowl combine the flour, baking soda, cinnamon, and salt. Mix well.
At low speed, slowly add the flour mixture and beat until batter is smooth.
Stir in carrots, pineapple, and whatever optional ingredients you have chosen.
Pour batter into prepared pan and bake at 350 degrees for 60–70 minutes. Insert cake tester to make sure center is done.
Let cake cool and frost with frosting recipe (following).
Makes 6–8 muffins.

Frosting

1½ packs vegan cream cheese, softened
1 cup confectioner's sugar
½ teaspoon vanilla extract
2 tablespoons soy milk

Method

Mix all ingredients with a hand mixer at high speed until well blended.

Carrot Oatmeal Squares

⅔ cup packed brown sugar
1 tablespoon canola oil
¾ cup nut milk
1 teaspoon vanilla extract
2 tablespoons cornstarch
¾ cup whole wheat flour
1½ cups rolled oats
2 teaspoons baking powder
1 teaspoon ground cinnamon
¼ teaspoon baking soda
¼ teaspoon salt
1 cup carrots, shredded
½ cup raisins
½ cup Craisins® (optional)
½ cup shredded coconut
Cooking spray

Method

Preheat oven to 350 degrees. Combine brown sugar, oil, milk, and vanilla and mix well. Add in flour and blend well. Now add all other ingredients and blend well. Pour into a greased 9x13-inch rectangular glass dish and bake 30–35 minutes, or until done. Insert cake tester to make sure center is done. To promote a moist texture, place a container with water in the oven on the bottom shelf during baking time. Cool and cut into squares.

Grilled Pineapple

Peel and cut 1 pineapple into long spears or round slices
1 tablespoon ginger root, peeled and grated
1 tablespoon brown sugar, optional

Method

Mix pineapple, sugar, and ginger together. Place pineapple spears on hot grill. Grill slowly until slightly browned and sugar has caramelized.

Bread Pudding

1 French or Italian bread loaf, cubed or torn apart with hand
2–3 cups soy milk
1 (20-ounce) can crushed pineapples with juice
1 stick melted margarine
1 cup brown sugar
½ cup tofu, pureed
1 teaspoon cinnamon
1 teaspoon nutmeg
1 teaspoon each vanilla and almond extracts

Method

Mix all ingredients together in a large bowl. Pour into a greased 9x13-inch rectangular pan and bake at 350 degrees until brown on top.

Strawberry Mold

2 boxes kosher strawberry gelatin
1½ cups hot water
1 (15-ounce) can crushed pineapple, drained
3 large ripe bananas, mashed
2 boxes fresh organic strawberries, washed and mashed
9 ounces vegan whipped cream

Method

Dissolve gelatin into hot water. Add pineapple, bananas, and strawberries.

Pour half the mixture into a glass container and let it set in refrigerator for about 2 hours.

Take out of refrigerator when set and add whipped cream layer, then the remaining gelatin mixture. Keep the second half of gelatin mixture at room temperature until the first half has set. Cover with plastic wrap and place back refrigerator to set overnight.

Cornmeal Muffins

Dry ingredients:
1 cup flour
⅔ cup cornmeal
¼ teaspoon salt
1 tablespoon baking powder
1 tablespoon cornstarch

Wet ingredients:
1½ sticks vegan margarine, melted
1 cup soy milk

Filling:
½ cup peach preserves

Method

Preheat oven to 400 degrees.

Grease muffin 6 tins. Sift together all dry ingredients and set aside.

Combine the wet ingredients in a bowl and slowly mix in dry ingredients with a wooden spoon.

Fill greased muffin tins halfway up to top with batter, spoon in a dollop of peach preserves, then fill muffin tin with the rest of batter to cover the filling.

Bake in the center of oven for 20 minutes. Allow to cool and then serve.

Cornbread

Dry ingredients:
1½ cups flour
1 cup cornmeal
1 tablespoon flaxseed meal
⅔ cup sugar
2 teaspoons baking powder
½ teaspoon salt

Wet ingredients:
½ cup milk of choice
⅓ cup canola oil
⅓ cup applesauce
1 can (14.75 oz.) creamed corn

Method

Preheat oven to 400 degrees. Grease an 11x7-inch baking pan. Whisk dry ingredients in one bowl. Combine wet ingredients in another bowl. Slowly mix dry ingredients into wet ingredients, but do not over stir. Pour into pan and bake for 30 minutes. Check for doneness with a toothpick.

Yellow Box Cake Surprise

1 box yellow moist deluxe cake mix
⅔ cup soy milk or buttermilk
1 stick margarine, softened
3 tablespoons corn starch
4 ounces white chocolate, melted
1 (8-ounce) can crushed pineapple, drained

Method

Follow instructions on box to mix the cake batter. Add melted chocolate and drained crushed pineapple to batter and bake following box instructions.

Scones

4 cups pastry flour
¼ cup sugar
4 tablespoons corn starch
2 tablespoons baking powder
1 cup Craisins®
½ teaspoon salt
3 sticks cold margarine, diced
½ teaspoon orange rind zest
1 cup nut milk (or heavy cream)

Method

Preheat oven to 400 degrees.
Place the flour, sugar, corn starch, baking powder, Craisins®, and salt in a mixing bowl. Combine well.

Blend in margarine with pastry knife.
Add the orange zest to the milk and add to flour mixture.
Using a fork, combine until blended into a ball.
Flour countertop and place dough ball on it.
With a rolling pin, gently roll out dough to ½-inch thickness.
Cut out in desired shapes and place on parchment paper-lined baking sheet.

Bake for 20–25 minutes.

Basic Flaky Jamaican Pastry Crust

4 cups all-purpose flour
3 sticks cold margarine
Ice cold water, about ½ cup

Method

Use pastry cutter to cut margarine into flour. Gently knead with fingertips while pouring cold water slowly. Cut into golf-ball sized pieces (for small pastries) and roll out into desired size and shape for your recipe.

Pastry Crust

4 cups spelt flour
3 sticks very cold vegan margarine
1 teaspoon turmeric powder
1 tablespoon brown sugar
⅓ cup cold water
½ teaspoon salt

Method

Place ingredients into food processor to make dough. Pulse until combined. Wrap dough in plastic wrap and then place refrigerator for 20 minutes before using. Always keep dough cold for best results.

Note: Add ice cubes to a larger second bowl and place working bowl into that to keep the dough cold.

Cookie Crust for Pies

1½ cups crumbled cookies of choice
1 stick vegan margarine, softened

Method

Blend together in a food processor or using a strong wooden spoon and press into a pie pan.

Soft Rolls

Heat 2 cups soy milk and mix with:
¼ cup vegan margarine
½ cup sugar
1½ teaspoons salt
Let cool after mixing.

Combine in a small bowl:
¼ cup lukewarm water
2 tablespoons active dry yeast
¼ teaspoon sugar
Let rest for 5 minutes.

Flour mixture:
4 cups whole wheat flour
2 ½ cups spelt or soft white flour

Method

Add cooled milk mixture to yeast mixture. Add 1½ cups spelt or white flour.

Beat 200 times and let it rest for 5–10 minutes. Add 4 cups whole wheat flour one cup at a time and beat well. Begin to mix with your hand.

Add the remaining flour to produce a consistency that can be turned out on a floured surface and knead for 5 minutes.

Place dough in a well-oiled bowl covered with a clean, damp cloth and let rise for 1 hour.

Punch dough down and form into several rolls. Place rolls onto an oiled cookie sheet and let rise ½ hour.

Bake at 375 degrees for about 20 minutes or until tops are brown.

Brush with margarine and enjoy.

Chapter 8

Seasonings and Spices

Spiritizer

The Life Gene

Devotional thought presented for the discussion topic on the Forum at GCE, "June 12, 2021."

In 1898 Felix Hoffman, a German chemist working for Bayer company, was able to modify salicylic acid to create acetylsalicylic acid, which he named "aspirin." It became a wonder drug. Used as an antipyretic (for fever), an anti-inflammatory (for swelling and redness), a pain reliever, and a very effective anticoagulant, aspirin today is still a miracle drug. And the real wonder and miracle about it is that it is available over the counter, inexplicably cheap.

Thirty-one years after the discovery of aspirin, penicillin was serendipitously discovered by a laboratory technician named Alexander Fleming. This led to the development of antibiotics treating such conditions as pneumonia, blood poisoning, strep throat, scarlet fever, diphtheria, syphilis, gonorrhea, meningitis, tonsilitis, and many more infectious diseases. Penicillin was really another wonder drug.

Just in case you have been wondering, there have been many more wonder drugs developed since, but they just don't make the news today like those did in past years. For example, recently, *Times of Israel* reported that Israeli scientists have discovered that they can increase the life expectancy of mice by 23 percent when they increase the supply of a protein named SIRT6. This protein normally decreases with age. (**https://1ref.us/23c**, accessed Oct. 25, 2022)

They are excited because if they can accomplish this in humans it would mean that you and I could live to an average age of 120 years, or more. And so, they are working on a drug that will increase the supply of this protein in humans. That would also be a wonder drug.

But a wonder drug for humans that perpetuates life has been given to us years ago. It is a combination product with two active ingredients—the body and the spirit. It was given to us when we were created by our Creator. The Lord put them together and voila—man became a living soul. Thus, man was gifted long life, forever.

> *A wonder drug for humans that perpetuates life has been given to us years ago.*

But sin interrupted and contaminated that formula, and since then man has been tirelessly trying to recreate or regain that life-sustaining, wonder drug. The good news is, that drug is available to us today. It comes from our Creator and is promised to us if we strive to know Him. "Now this is eternal life: that they know you, the only true God, and Jesus Christ, whom you have sent" (John 17:3, NIV). We might not have the state of immortality right now, but it is promised if we seek to know our Creator.

Look, do you want to live longer and live forever? Begin to know God and His Son, Jesus Christ, whom He sent to be our Savior, Mediator, and our eternal Life-Giver. He will infuse the wonder drug of life in us. That which we have right now may wean below therapeutic concentration and we die, or more appropriately, sleep, but Jesus will give us a life-everlasting dose, soon. Hold tight!

Eden's Hope Seasoning Mix

2 cups nutritional yeast
1 tablespoon sea salt
1 tablespoon onion powder
1 tablespoon garlic powder
1 tablespoon smoked paprika
1 tablespoon tarragon leaves
1 tablespoon dried thyme leaves
1 teaspoon turmeric

Method

Combine all ingredients in a plastic zipper bag and shake well. Label bag and use for all seasoning needs.

Sesame Parmesan Seasoning

½ cup toasted sesame seeds
½ cup nutritional yeast
1 tablespoon onion powder
¼ teaspoon garlic powder
½–1 teaspoon salt

Method

Blend well and store in a dry, sealed container or spice bottle.

Homemade Dry Spice

4 tablespoons fennel seeds
2 teaspoons anise seeds
1¼ teaspoons whole cloves
2 cinnamon sticks, broken in pieces
½ teaspoon ginger powder

Method

Place all ingredient in a blender and blend into fine powder. Store in a dry place.

Use ¼ teaspoon in recipes where mixed spice is needed.

Great in hot chocolate.

Chicken-Style Seasoning

2 cups nutritional yeast
2 teaspoons smoked paprika
2 tablespoons garlic powder
3 tablespoons onion granules
1 tablespoons marjoram
2 tablespoons dried thyme leaves
2 tablespoons kosher salt (use less if salt sensitive)
1 tablespoons sage
2 tablespoons dried parsley
1½ teaspoon celery seeds

Method

Mix all ingredients well and store into a labeled glass container. Use in any recipe calling for chicken-style seasoning.

Fish-Style Seasoning

1 tablespoon dulse or kelp powder
1 cup nutritional yeast
1 teaspoon celery seeds
2 tablespoons onion powder
1 tablespoon garlic powder

Method

Combine well, pour into a labeled glass container, and store in a dry place.

Curry Mix

3 tablespoons Jamaican curry powder
2 tablespoons sage
2 tablespoons vegetarian chicken-style seasoning mix
1 tablespoon garlic granules
2 tablespoons onion granules
3 tablespoons fresh thyme leaves
1 tablespoon ginger powder
1 tablespoon smoked paprika
4 tablespoons nutritional yeast
1 teaspoon sea salt
1 teaspoon crushed red pepper flakes, optional
1 cup coconut oil

Method

Combine ingredients well and Store in a glass bottle in a cool, dry place with your other seasonings. Use as a great substitute for chicken-style seasoning with a hit of curry flavor.

Chapter 9

Miscellaneous

Spiritizer

Higher Immunity

Our immune system is designed to keep us from getting sick or to help us recover from certain illnesses, usually from an invading agent. Our cells, tissues, organs, and body systems work together to accomplish this goal.

When a pathogen (a disease-causing agent such a virus, bacterium, fungi, protozoa, or a worm) enters our body, the body responds by producing antibodies that fight against and destroy that germ. Furthermore, the body remembers the make-up of the germ so that it can be better prepared to neutralize and destroy it, should there be an encounter in the future.

Sometimes, though, the body might not be able to act or react quickly enough to ward off the germ. And in the case where the germ multiplies rapidly, or the body is immunocompromised due to, for instance, medications that weaken the immune system (like immunosuppressants given after organ or bone morrow transplant or some medical treatments like cancer regimen), it can easily succumb to the effects of these invaders. This can lead to serious ailments or even death.

This is where vaccines come in. The idea and science of vaccines is to previously expose the body to a weakened, or killed, form of the germ that does not result in sickness, but instead causes the body to produce the defense antibodies against this particular pathogen. This way, when the real, live, or viable germ enters the body it is prepared for it. This is basically how vaccines provide immunity. It is usually much safer to get a vaccine than to get the disease it is designed to prevent.

This brings Hebrews 4:15 (NASB 1995) to my mind: "For we do not have a high priest who cannot sympathize with our weaknesses, but One who has been tempted in all things as we are, yet without sin."

It's like Jesus has already provided the immunity for sin. Pathogenic sin, in all its antigenic forms—lust of the eye, lust of the flesh, pride of life—approached Jesus and He resisted it in all its forms and developed antibodies against them all for us all.

"Christ was treated as we deserve that we may be treated as He deserves. He was condemned for our sins, in which He had no share, that we might be justified by His righteousness, in which we had no share. He suffered the death, which was ours, that we might receive the life which was His. 'By His stripes we are healed'" (Ellen G. White, *The Desire of the Ages*, p. 25).

> *It's like Jesus has already provided the immunity for sin.*

Jesus can provide inoculations for all sin problems.

You might be cautious, and even suspicious, of pharmaceutical vaccines, and maybe, rightly so. That's ok, but be sure to be judicious and auspicious about spiritual vaccination. It provides eternal life.

Father, thank You for the life You provide for us through Your Son, Jesus, who died on the cross. Amen!

Parmesan Cheeze

1 cup raw cashews or blanched almonds, rinsed and dried
4 tablespoons nutritional yeast
1 tablespoon garlic granules
1 tablespoon onion granules
1 teaspoon Himalayan pink salt
1 tablespoon lemon juice

Method

Put all ingredients except lemon juice into a food processor and blend until fine. Add lemon juice and pulse a few times to blend in. Store in a dry glass container inside your refrigerator.

Garlic Bread

½ cup margarine, softened
2 tablespoons vegan mayonnaise, optional
4 cloves garlic, finely minced
1 tablespoon dried parsley
½ cup nutritional yeast
1 loaf multi-grain French or Italian bread

Method

Combine all spread ingredients together in a bowl and mix well. Spread over bread.
Place buttered side up in oven at 350 degrees for a few minutes until edge of bread is brown.

Sweet Potato Sticks

> Wash and peel desired amount of sweet potatoes and cut into thick sticks. Place in a bowl and coat thoroughly with olive oil. Sprinkle with your favorite seasonings and spread out on a cookie sheet.
>
> Bake at 350 degrees for 30 minutes. Remove from oven, turn over to other side, and continue baking another 20–30 minutes, or until desired color. Drizzle with honey and cinnamon, or dip into cashew cream.

Hash Browns

> Select yellow Yukon gold potatoes and wash well, leaving skin on. Shred and season with black pepper and chicken-style seasoning. Heap onto a greased waffle skillet and fry until golden brown.

Turned Corn Meal

¼ cup green bell pepper, diced
¼ cup red bell pepper, diced
¼ cup onion, diced
1 stick butter or margarine
1 cup fine corn meal
2 quarts boiling coconut milk
1 teaspoon salt

Method

Sauté peppers and onions with butter until soft and set aside.

Moisten corn meal with a little cold water and stir into salted boiling coconut milk.

Add sautéed peppers and onions and cook over low heat, stirring all the while until done. This can be eaten at this point, OR—

Pour hot meal into a greased glass dish and smooth out. Let sit uncovered until cold and firm. Cut into wedges, dip into seasoned flour, and fry in hot oil until brown on all sides.

Serve with syrup as a breakfast item, or with an entrée for lunch or dinner.

Corn Pudding

1 (15-ounce) can whole kernel corn
1 pound firm tofu, pureed
1 cup nut milk
2 tablespoons flour
2 tablespoons sugar
3 tablespoons butter, melted
Salt and pepper to taste

Method

Place all ingredients into one bowl and mix well.

Pour in a greased 8x8-inch casserole dish and bake at 300 degrees for 1 hour.

Mini Cheese Pizzas

1 can Grands® flaky refrigerated biscuits
⅓ cup tomato sauce or spaghetti sauce
½ teaspoon dried oregano leaves
½ cup vegan shredded mozzarella cheese

Method

Preheat oven to 350 degrees. Pat each biscuit out into a 4-inch circle on a baking sheet coated with nonstick cooking spray. In a small bowl, mix together the sauce and oregano. Spoon the sauce onto each biscuit round and sprinkle with cheese. Bake at 350 degrees for 10 minutes, or until cheese is melted.

Note: You may substitute English muffins or bagels for Grands® flaky biscuits.

Tofu Spinach Triangles

1 pound firm tofu, drained and mashed
2 cups frozen spinach, thawed and drained of all water
½ cup vegetarian meat of choice, chopped
1 pack wonton wrappers
Pesto sauce (see p. 145 for recipe)

Method

Mix together tofu, spinach, and chopped vegetarian meat of choice.

Place 1½ teaspoons of spinach mixture on each wonton wrapper and seal in the shape of a triangle using water on the edges. Drop a few at a time into boiling water and cook for one to two minutes.

Remove from pan and place in a bowl.

Pour prepared pesto sauce over them and enjoy.

Note: You may also deep fry the triangles.

Jerked Tofu

1 pound firm tofu
1 tablespoon Jamaican jerk season
1 medium onion, chopped
2 stalks scallion, chopped
1 teaspoon fresh thyme
1 tablespoon nutritional yeast
1 tablespoon vegetarian chicken-style seasoning
1 tablespoon olive oil
Dash of low salt soy sauce

Method

Cut tofu into 1-inch cubes and place along with all the seasonings into a shallow glass dish. With a spatula, gently toss everything until seasonings are thoroughly mixed with tofu. Cover with foil. Place into preheated oven at 400 degrees and bake for 30 minutes.

Remove cover and continue cooking until edges are brown.

Turn tofu a few times so pieces are brown on all sides.

Tofu Jerky

1 pound extra firm tofu
1 tablespoon nutritional yeast
1 tablespoon soy sauce
1 tablespoon Jamaican jerk seasoning
1 tablespoon vegetarian chicken-style seasoning
2 cloves garlic, crushed
2 tablespoons favorite marinating sauce
Cooking spray

Method

Slice tofu block in half, then make slices of each half (about ⅛-inch). Do not cut too thin.

Place all seasonings into a large plastic zipper bag and gently add tofu to bag, trying not to break the pieces.

Carefully turn bag over a few times to ensure seasoning gets on each piece of tofu.

Seal bag and place in refrigerator overnight or for 24 hours.

Turn bag over every time you go to the refrigerator, or each time you remember.

Spray cookie sheet with cooking spray and place tofu side by side on sheet.

Spray the side facing up and bake in a 350-degree oven.

Keep turning tofu every 20 minutes to make sure it is getting brown and dry, but not burnt. This should take about 45 minutes. Place finished product into a clean, dry Ziploc® bag or glass container with cover while hot, and seal.

Enjoy as a snack.

Note: Placing the hot product in a bag or container with cover locks in the moisture as it cools, giving a better chewy texture to the tofu.

Homemade Coconut Milk

1 large dry coconut
4 cups warm water

Method

Break coconut in small pieces and remove white, firm flesh from husk (make sure coconut is not spoiled). Place coconut pieces into blender with warm water in batches and blend well. Strain milk through a large strainer into a bowl.

Repeat process until all milk has been expressed (when milk is no longer white and creamy).

Tofu Rung Dung (Jamaican Style)

2 stalks green onion, chopped
½ cup red onion, chopped
2 tablespoons coconut oil
¼ teaspoon turmeric
1 pound firm tofu, cut in cubes and lightly browned in frying pan
1 package coconut powder + 2 cups water (or 2 cups milk expressed from 1 coconut)
1 sprig fresh thyme
2 cloves garlic, pressed or minced
2 vegetarian bouillon cube (or 2 teaspoons vegan seasoning)
2 tablespoons nutritional yeast

Method

Sauté onions and garlic with coconut oil and turmeric. Add water, thyme, and bouillon cubes to the coconut powder/water mixture (or fresh coconut milk) and simmer for a few minutes. Add tofu and nutritional yeast. Let simmer until most of the liquid has evaporated. Add more seasoning if needed.

Chapter 10

Tasty This and That

Spiritizer

Of All Nations, Peoples, and Tongues

Have you ever had a dream?

"Many times," I hear you say. Well, I had one recently. I dreamt Jesus returned and I went to heaven. It was the most magnificent place I have ever seen. It was dazzling with indescribable beauty.

After the initial shock of my making it there, I sang "Hallelujah to the Lamb." I then decided to do a tour and explore the place. Since I am originally from Jamaica, I decided to visit the Jamaican section. I searched, and searched, and searched, but I could not find it.

So, I thought, "Ok, maybe they are included in the African American section. Let me go find them." I searched, and searched, and searched again. I could not find them—I could not find that section.

So, I said, "Ok, I know, let me visit the white people's section. Surely, there must be a section like that. Let me see who is included there. To my surprise, there was no Caucasian section. I just could not find it. So, I looked around with keen observance to see who were really there.

And after careful observation, I noticed that there was just one race there. It was the human race. It was such a magnificent blend so that no ethnicity was prominent above the other. Just one race—the redeemed of God and the Lamb, Jesus, singing the glorious anthem: "Redeemed how I love to proclaim it. Redeemed by the blood of the lamb."

Today you will hear the popular slogan: "Black lives matter." And they surely do, but to me the slogan should be more inclusive. We should make it include everyone by saying something like: Black lives matter too, or Black lives matter as well.

When we concentrate on ourselves mainly, we stand the chance of forgetting others. It has happened in the past, and it is happening now.

And by the way, what color is God? Ezekiel was one of those who got a glimpse of Him and told us about it. He said that all he could see was the brightness of God's glory surrounding God. And what did it look like? It was like the rainbow that appears after the rain. What color is the rainbow? a combination of seven prominent colors that incorporates all the other colors in the spectrum.

Yes, your God and my God is a God of all people, race, and color.

Luke, the physician, says that God made all nations of one blood, all to live on the face of the earth. And He even determined where they should live (Acts 17:26). This is no coincidence. Luke gives a reason for this too: That they should seek the Lord and find Him. For in Him we live and move and find our existence (Acts 17:26–28).

> *When we concentrate on ourselves mainly, we stand the chance of forgetting others.*

Wow! So, it seems like the diversity of peoples, nations, and languages is for the main reason of us seeking after our Creator, finding Him, and ultimately giving Him praise and honor because we were all created by Him, and for Him, and in Him all things hold together and exist.

So, brothers and sisters of all ethnicities, cultures, and races, what are we waiting for? Let's just praise the LORD!

Steamed Callaloo

Prepare by stripping off outer film from stalks of fresh callaloo and then cut up the callaloo into small-sized pieces as you would collard greens. (Fresh is better, but you may purchase the canned callaloo instead.)
Cut up one medium onion, one medium tomato, and one small red pepper.
Seasoning to taste
¼ cup coconut milk
2 tablespoons oil

Method

Sauté onions, peppers, and tomatoes in oil. Add coconut milk. Place callaloo into pot and do not cover. Cook until soft and liquid has been absorbed.

Tomatoes and Peaches

Diced tomatoes (you may substitute carrots)
Diced peaches
Salt to taste
Oil

Method

Place all into a pot and cook together until the juices from the fruits thicken.

Green Banana/Plantain Balls in Peanut Stew

Peel and cut bananas or plantains and cook in salted water.

Mash with fork or potato masher and form into balls with your hands when cool enough. Place into peanut sauce (see recipe on p. 122) and simmer.

Cornmeal Mush

¼ cup green bell pepper and red bell pepper, diced
3 cloves garlic, crushed
1 tablespoon coconut oil
1½ cups yellow cornmeal
3 cups coconut milk
1 teaspoon fresh thyme leaves

Method

Sauté peppers and garlic in oil over medium heat in a saucepan. Add milk and bring to boil. Turn off heat and slowly stir in cornmeal to avoid clumping. Stir until all cornmeal is added and any lumps are gone. Return to low heat and cook for 10 minutes.

Sour Cream

1 pound tofu, firm
Juice from 1 large lemon
1 teaspoon honey
½ teaspoon sea salt
3 tablespoons oil

Method

Place all ingredients in blender and blend until smooth and creamy in consistency.

Deli Slices

½ cup old fashioned rolled oats
3 cups Ritz® crackers
1 cup raw cashews
3 cups coconut milk
2 teaspoons vegetarian chicken-style seasoning

Method

Place all ingredients into blender and blend until smooth. Grease clean soup cans and pour blended ingredients into them. Cover with foil and secure with rubber band. Steam for 2 hours in a double boiler on the stovetop. Allow to cool before slicing very thin for sandwiches.

Pakasah

Boil 6 peeled, green bananas, 2 pounds eddoes or African yams with 4 cups fresh coconut milk until liquid is almost gone from pot. Add curry, onions, crushed garlic, salt and other seasons to taste during cooking.

This is a one pot meal; you may add anything you desire into pot.

Note: If you have a background of Caribbean or African heritage, this is known as comfort food when the groceries are low and there is not much to cook.

Grilled/Roasted Ripe Plantains

Wash ripe plantains and roast with skin on a hot grill. Take out of skin when done and pour favorite chutney all over and serve.

Tofu Ricotta

2 pounds extra firm tofu, drained and pressed
2 tablespoons Ener-G® egg replacer
¼ cup fresh squeezed lemon juice
2½ tablespoons oil
1 teaspoon basil
1 teaspoon salt

Method

Shred pressed tofu on box grater, then mix in other ingredients.

Curried Vegetables

Cut up vegetables of choice (carrots, pumpkin, green beans, spinach, etc.)
1 cup white potatoes, diced
1 cup green beans
1 cup pumpkin
1 small onion, chopped
½ cup frozen green peas
1 teaspoon curry powder
Pinch of salt
1 teaspoon chicken-style seasoning
4 cups fresh coconut milk (or 2 cans plus 1 cup of water—add more if desired.

Method

Place all ingredients into a pot and pour enough coconut milk over contents to cover about 2 inches. Cook until all ingredients are soft.

Amaranth and Millet

May be cooked like rice. Begin with 1 cup of one of these grains, wash, then add water to 1 inch above grains in a 2-quart saucepan. Cook for 30 minutes then fluff with fork.

Fried Cassava/White Yam

Peel and cut desired amount of cassava or yam into small pieces
Salt to taste
Oil for frying

Method

Place cassava or yam in a bowl and sprinkle with salt. Heat oil and fry bite size cassava/yam pieces until done. Serve with tomato sauce (see recipe p. 123)

Juicy Fruit Salad

Pineapples
Peaches
Plums
Ripe mangoes
Honey or maple syrup, optional
Lemon or lime juice

Method

Wash, peel, and cut all fruits into bite size pieces and place into a large bowl. Squeeze lemon juice all over fruit salad and drizzle with honey or maple syrup. Serve same day.

Cassava with Coconut Milk

4 cups peeled and sliced cassava
1 coconut, expressed with water to produce 4 cups of milk (see recipe p. 174)
¼ cup sugar or honey

Method

Place milk and cassava into pot and cook over low heat.

Add sugar when contents inside pot have thickened. Eat as a desert.

Note: You can omit the sweetener and add seasoning and salt to taste following the same process for a more savory treat.

Chapter 11

Helpful Tips and More...

- Use cooked, frozen foods within one month.
- Label each container with date before freezing leftovers.
- Never refreeze food once it has been thawed.
- To avoid teary eyes when cutting onions, cut in half and immerse them in water after peeling.
- Fill up your garbage disposal with ice cubes and run it to sharpen the blades.
- Parchment paper provides an excellent nonstick surface when baking.
- Nuts and grains keep best and longer when kept in freezer. They do not freeze so may be used directly from freezer when needed. Grains may be kept up to 5 months in the freezer.
- Make an extra batch of your favorite casserole for freezing and use within 2 months.
- Place a wooden spoon across pot when cooking pasta to avoid the mess of it boiling over onto stove top.
- Place wooden spoon handle into oil in skillet or stove. If bubbles form around the handle, the oil is hot enough to begin frying. Also, if you added too much salt to your soup or sauce pot, add a layer of raw, white potato slices on the top. When the slices are cooked, remove them and discard. The salt will be absorbed by the potatoes.
- Wash vegetables before cutting to avoid losing their nutritional value down the drain.
- Add a little fresh lemon juice to simmering rice to help keep grains separated.
- Add salt towards the end of cooking beans and corn to avoid them being tough after cooking.

- Place one or two lettuce leaves to top of soup pot to absorb excess grease.
- Lemon juice and water will bring soggy lettuce leaves back to life.
- Use an egg slicer to slice soft fruits such as bananas and strawberries when making fruit salad.

Cloves—Good in sweet dishes; contains soothing essential oils and antiseptic properties. Good for toothaches.

Nutmeg—Helps to relieve pain and soothe indigestion. Excellent in dishes with squashes/pumpkins.

Cumin—Very versatile, may be used as powder or whole seeds; good in curries, stews, and dips.

Cayenne pepper—Aids in blood circulation.

Coriander—May be used in sweet and savory dishes; mixes well with cumin and turmeric.

Turmeric—Powerful anti-inflammatory and antioxidant effects; adds beautiful color to rice dishes.

Fresh, fundamental base flavors to build other ingredients on when cooking savory dishes:

Ginger	Brings spice and zest
Lemons	Storehouse of vitamin C
Chilies	Helps to digest food faster
Garlic	Flavor agent
Onion	Boosts all the other flavors

If you must have a sweetener, omit the processed sugar and try one of these:

Pureed Date
Raisins
Maple syrup
Agave
Raw honey
Molasses
Organic Apple juice
Home grown stevia leaves

Best oils for frying/sautéing:

Unrefined coconut oil
Rice bran oil
Grapeseed oil

Applesauce—May be used instead of oil in baking cakes, cookies, other sweet treats.

Arrowroot and Corn starch powder—Use to thicken soups, sauces, stews, and gravies. It is also a great substitute for eggs in baking. If allergic to corn, use the arrowroot.

Aqua Faba—This is the new vegan's best friend to make whipped cream; egg white substitute for baking and meringue.

Garbanzo Water—You may use the juice from the garbanzo bean can or make your own. Best used for whipping when cold.

Spiritizer

The Pandemic

During the SARS-CoV-2 (Covid-19) pandemic we experienced shortages of commodities, food items, medical supplies, and a slew of other things. In the pharmacy scarce items included hand sanitizers, latex and vinyl gloves, disinfectants, rubbing alcohol, alcohol swabs, face masks, cough and cold products (zinc lozenges, decongestants, and cough suppressants), and even certain prescription items. Added to that list were thermometers and a special device called the pulse oximeter.

The pulse oximeter is a device used to non-invasively and painlessly measure the oxygen level in a person's blood when the index finger is inserted in it. It specifically measures the percentage of blood hemoglobin carrying oxygen. This is called the oxygen saturation percentage (SpO^2), and the procedure is called pulse oximetry.

Obtaining vital signs is an essential tool for monitoring hospitalized patients (or anyone for that matter) because changes in their vital signs can be a precursor to clinical deterioration. Monitoring vital signs, therefore, can lead to timely intervention that can prevent or mitigate serious medical outcomes.

The common vital signs are body temperature, pulse rate, heart rate, respiration rate, and blood pressure. But oxygen saturation is now considered by many to be an additional vital sign—especially during the Covid-19 pandemic—because low oxygen levels can be an indication that medical intervention is needed, even if the person is not feeling ill.

Normal SpO^2 is within the range of 90–95%. But a person with Covid-19 and a SpO^2 level under 85% should consult their physician immediately as this could be a sign of medical decline.

The treatment of choice for low oxygen saturation (SpO^2, of 85% or lower) is, of course, the administration of oxygen. I am wondering if I could say that the

Word (Scripture) and prayer could be considered as the spiritual oximetry for the soul.

The Word itself seems to indicate that our involvement in both Scripture and prayer gives an indication of how spiritually saturated we are.

The WORD:

Ps. 119:38 (ESV): My soul melts away from sorrow; strengthen me according to your word.

Ps. 119: 111 (ESV): Your testimonies are ... the joy of my heart.

Ps. 119: 130 (ESV): The unfolding of your words gives light; it imparts understanding to the simple.

Matt. 4:4 (AKJV): Man shall not live by bread alone but by every word that proceedeth out of the mouth of God.

And Prayer:

Phil. 4:6, 7 (NIV): Do not be anxious about anything, but in every situation, by prayer and petition, with thanksgiving, present your requests to God. And the peace of God, which transcends all understanding, will guard your hearts and your minds in Christ Jesus.

1 Thess. 5:16–18 (NIV): Rejoice always, pray continually, give thanks in all circumstances; for this is God's will for you in Christ Jesus.

The scripture is replete with promises of not just spiritual, but physical, social, mental, and even environmental benefits for those who study the Word of God and indulge themselves in prayer.

Here is a favorite text of mine: 2 Chronicles 7:14 (NIV): "If my people, who are called by my name, will humble themselves and pray and seek my face and turn from their wicked ways, then I will hear from heaven, and I will forgive their sin and will heal their land."

Do you want to experience peace of mind in this troubled world and ultimate robust health and longevity in the future? Then saturate your soul with the Word of God and prayer.

Chapter 12

Pantry/Freezer Items for "Drop-On" Guests

Big Franks® (canned hot dogs)
Deli slices (frozen)
Vegenaise® or any vegan mayonnaise
Vegetarian chili (canned)
Canned beans (variety)
Fripats®/Grillers®/chicken patties (frozen)
Vegetarian corn dogs (frozen)
Vegetarian shredded cheddar and sliced cheese
Burger and hot dog buns, multigrain bread

These above meat alternative products may be found in your local Adventist Health Food store.

- Big Franks® may be used for quick hot dogs, chili dogs, or cut franks into small pieces and sauté with vegetables or add to scrambled tofu.
- Sauté onions, peppers, and ketchup with one or two sliced Big Franks®.
- Spread multigrain bread with vegan mayonnaise. Add deli slices, tomatoes, and lettuce.
- Heat Fripats® or Grillers® in toaster oven and place on bun with toppings for burger.
- Cut Grillers®/Fripats®/chicken patties in strips. Add to sautéed onions and green peppers with seasonings for fajitas. Wrap in tortilla.
- Place Grillers® or Fripats® into shallow pan and pour favorite BBQ sauce over patties and simmer.
- Bake Dinner Roast® according to instructions on package and keep in fridge. Slice for quick sandwiches, topping for salads, or add to gravy. Delicious with baked potatoes.
- Use vegetarian cheese for grilled cheese sandwiches, quesadillas, or topping for baked potatoes.

Spiritizer

The Panacean Drug

Did you know that there are over 20,000 pharmaceutical agents (drugs or medicines) approved for use in the United States? (**https://1ref.us/23d**, accessed Oct. 25, 2022)

Try to add to this list the over-the-counter (OTC) agents such as minerals, vitamins, herbs, and phytochemicals and we will get a staggering number of over 300,000 therapeutic agents.

There are so many OTC agents available alone, that the U.S. Food and Drug Administration (FDA) simply groups them into about 80 therapeutics categories, monitoring only their ingredients and labelling. Their quality, quantity, and purity can be dubious.

There are pharmaceutical agents for A—abscess, B—boils, C—cancer, D—diabetes. Let's just say that there are agents available—both prescription and OTC—for conditions A to Z, and repeated multiple times over.

Some of these agents are wonderful chemicals that prevent, mitigate, treat, or even heal many maladies; but some are bad agents that can maim or even kill. And even the "safe" ones can cause untoward effects if not taken as intended.

So, if you are taking any medication and have questions, please check with your physician, pharmacist, or other health professionals for advice. Because there is one sure thing about these agents—good or bad—they can all lend to potential side effects, adverse effects, contraindications, and even death.

So, I am occasionally asked: "Doc, is there a medicine that I can take that has no side effects, no adverse effects, no contraindications?"

I would instinctively say, "Yes." And I would add that such a drug also has no dosage limitations or expiration dates.

Then they would ask for the name of the drug and where they could find it. Here is where I would point them to the text John 17:3 (KJV): "And this is life eternal, that they might know thee the only true God, and Jesus Christ, whom thou hast sent."

And I would say: "There it is. There He is. Jesus!"

And usually they would say something like: "Come on, Jesus?"

And I would respond: "Yes, Jesus!" Like the song says:

> The mere mention of His name,
>
> Can calm the storm, heal the broken, raise the dead,
>
> At the name of Jesus I've seen sin hardened men melted,
>
> Derelicts transformed,
>
> Emperors have tried to destroy it,
>
> Philosophies have tried to stamp it out,
>
> Tyrants have tried to wash it from the face of the Earth,
>
> With the very blood of those who claimed it.

Then I would add: "But the name of Jesus stands unerasable, leaving indelible impressions on the minds and hearts of those who are willing to call His name—Jesus."

And so, my friends, Jesus—the panacea of all drugs—stands and asks: "What can I do for you?"

> **The name of Jesus stands unerasable, leaving indelible impressions on the minds and hearts of those who are willing to call His name—Jesus**

Are you hungry? Do you need bread? I am the Bread of Life.

Are you thirsty? Do you need water? I am the Living Water.

Are you sick? Do you need healing? I am the Great Physician.

And by the way, you are a sinner and you need salvation; I am your Savior.

And so, as a pharmacist, may I dispense Jesus to you? He is the best medicine I know. Take Him five times a day: morning, noon, evening, at bedtime, and PRN—as often as is needed.

Your medication is now dispensed! TAKE AS INSTRUCTED.

Chapter 13

Still Something More...

Perfect health requires perfect circulation

Yogurt Cleanser

1 cup plain yogurt
2 tablespoons safflower oil
3 teaspoons fresh squeezed lemon/lime juice

Method

Mix ingredients well and store inside refrigerator.
Pour small amount into palm and massage your skin gently (if using on face, avoid eye area).
Rinse with water and pat dry.

Foaming Hand Soap

1 empty soap bottle with pump
¼ cup liquid hand soap
Drops of peppermint oil
Distilled water to fill bottle (leave 1–2 inches for space to shake contents)

Method

Pour ingredients into bottle, put on pump, and shake.

Facial Masks for Oily Skin

Mashed ripe avocados (moisturizes the skin)
Mashed strawberries (rids the skin of dead cells)
Grated cucumber (soothing for sunburns)
Mayonnaise (improves and conditions skin texture)
Plain yogurt (rich in protein, calcium, and vitamins)
Mashed tomatoes (effective on blackheads and oily skin; deep-cleans skin's surface)

<u>Use them interchangeably as you desire.</u>
Best to be lying flat when mask is applied—even better when applied for you by someone else!

Avocado Seed Scrub

<u>2 avocado seeds, washed and dried</u>

Wrap each seed in paper towels and place into a plastic zipper bag, expelling all of the air.
Use a hammer and pound the seeds into pea-size pieces.
Spread crushed pieces onto a cookie sheet and allow to air dry for a few days in open air.
Place in a coffee grinder or food processor and grind fine.
Place onto a cookie sheet and allow to air dry completely once more.
When dry, place in a plastic zipper bag and store.
Add this to your liquid soap or cream and use on your skin to exfoliate.

Face Cream

4 tablespoons petroleum jelly
4 tablespoons shea or cocoa butter
4 tablespoons organic unrefined coconut oil

Method

Mix all together in a glass measuring cup.

Place glass container into a pan with water on stove, and heat slowly to melt.

Pour immediately into a clean container, and allow to cool completely.

Contents will solidify when cool.

Massage into face, especially around eyes and mouth. Cream is very rich so only a small amount is needed.

Lip Gloss

2 teaspoons organic unrefined coconut oil
2 teaspoons petroleum jelly

Method

Mix together and place in microwave at full power for 1 minute (or place into a water bath on stove top, warm slowly until melted).

Pour into a clean container and let cool.

Use as lip gloss.

Sleep Aid

1 tablespoon unrefined coconut oil
¼ tablespoon honey
Pinch of sea salt

Method

Combine well and drink. You may also add to ½ cup of warm water and drink before going to bed.

Bloat Relief

½ ripe banana
1 teaspoon crushed almonds
½ cup almond milk
½ teaspoon cinnamon powder
½ teaspoon grated ginger

Method

Blend with a spoon and enjoy.

Muscle Soother

1 cup sea salt
1 cup baking soda
1 cup Epsom salt

Method

Mix all ingredients together and store in dry place.
Use: After a physically hard day—
Pour ½ cup of mixture into bathtub of warm water and allow to dissolve.
Soak in tub and feel the muscles relax.
Massage body with cream or oil after soak to replace moisture into skin.

Deodorant

1 tablespoon baking soda
2 drops lemon extract

Method

Mix well together and smear a small amount under arm.

Salt Rub

2 cups coarse salt
1 cup olive or safflower oil

Method

Mix together into a thick paste and pour into a clean container (will keep up to 2 months without refrigeration).

Lather up with your regular soap and wash off as usual.

While standing in the shower, scoop a handful of paste and gently rub into skin (do not use on face or broken skin).

Be very careful when rubbing feet because you might slip and fall.

Rinse off with warm water and pat dry with clean towel.

You will not want to wash off the moisturizing oil.

The salt removes dead surface cells at the same time the oil lubricates the skin.

Natural Laxatives

1 cup chopped prunes
1 cup chopped dates
5 cups boiling water

Method

Boil together on low fire until thick.

Drink ¼ before bedtime.

---

1 cup prunes
½ cups dried figs

Method

Soak together in 32 ounces of distilled water.
Blend until smooth.
Drink 8 ounces each night before bed.

Flu Bomb

2 cloves garlic, crushed
½ teaspoons fresh grated ginger
Juice of one lemon
1 drop eucalyptus oil
1 teaspoon honey
½ cup water
Dash cayenne pepper

Method

Blend with a spoon and drink two times daily.

Hair Nourishment

¼ cup mayonnaise
¼ cup ripe avocado, mashed

Method

Add more of each ingredient depending on length of hair.
Massage into clean towel-dried h air after shampooing.
Cover with a plastic shower cap and let it sit for 15 minutes.
Rinse hair with cool water and dry as usual.

Blood Builder

64 ounces unfiltered grape juice
1 cup prune juice
1 cup molasses
1 cup each raisins and figs soaked in 1 cup water then pureed

Method
Blend well together in a blender and leave on counter overnight. Refrigerate next morning. Drink 4 ounces three times per day for 7 days.

Toothpaste

2 tablespoons coconut oil
1 tablespoon baking soda
15 drops peppermint oil
1 packet stevia

Method
Mix and store in an airtight container. Use as needed.

Quick Mouth Fresheners

Fresh parsley, mint, grated ginger, fennel seeds, anise seeds

Method

Keep seeds handy if you plan to eat out.

Eat the fresh parsley or mint garnish from your plate.

Mix 1 cup warm water and 1 teaspoon sea salt.

Gargle to rid mouth of bacteria or heal sore gums (do not swallow).

Teeth Cleaners/Whitener

1 teaspoon baking soda mixed with 1 teaspoon activated charcoal powder.

Charcoal Poultice

2 tablespoons activated charcoal powder
2 tablespoons psyllium husks or flax seed meal
3–4 tablespoons warm water (more if desired to make a paste)
¼ teaspoon cayenne pepper
1 large plastic zipper bag

Place ingredients into plastic zipper bag and knead gently with hand until a mound is formed. Place bag on counter and roll poultice flat with a rolling pin.

Fold and keep in freezer or refrigerator until needed. Cut to fit size of area to be treated. Remove top layer of plastic and place poultice on skin. Wrap with plastic wrap and gauze.

Charcoal neutralizes and adsorbs poison

Resources

Vegetarian food may be found in most health food stores or online.

Registered dietitians may be found at: Freelancedietition.org and https://1ref.us/23e.

Attend an Eden's Hope Ministries health workshop and experience first-hand how fascinating and joyful living a healthy lifestyle can be. Healthy cooking vegetarian/vegan cooking classes: https://Edenshopeministries.com.

Your guide to food additives: https://1ref.us/23h.

Your guide to the dirty dozen and clean 15 fruits and vegetables: https://1ref.us/23f.

Condensed milk and vegan tuna source: https://1ref.us/23g.

References

Radd, S. *Food As Medicine*. Signs Publishing Company, 2016.

Walker, Carolle Hester. *Healthful Living Cookbook*. TEACH Services, Inc., 2015.

Index

A

Açaí Bowl 40
Amaranth and Millet 182
Apple Tortilla Delite 30
Apricot Chickett* 97
Apricot Glazed Gluten 98

B

Baked Burrito 94
Banana Bran Muffin 152
Banana Bread 1 153
Banana Bread 2 153
Banana Jackfruit Ice Cream 47
Banana Yogurt and Berries 23
Bean Fritters 32
Better Than Butter 28
Beverages
    Beet Drink 58
    Cold or Hot Chai 57
    Cucumber Drink 56
    Ginger Tea 59
    Hawaiian Lemonade for a Crowd 56
    Hot Peanut Butter Tea 58
    Spiced Chai Mix 56
Bread Pudding 156
Broccoli Casserole 116
Buckwheat Breakfast Burritos 24

C

Carrot and Nut Sandwich	135
Carrot Cake/Muffins	154
Carrot Oatmeal Squares	155
Cashew Vegan Mayo	142
Cassava with Coconut Milk	183
Cheese Casserole	115
Chili Mac	116
Coconut Yogurt	39
Confetti Scramble	19
Corn Pudding	171
Cornbread	158
Cornmeal Muffins	157
Cornmeal Mush	179
Cornmeal Porridge	42
Cottage Cheese Nut Loaf	98
Crazy Hoagie	132
Cream Cheese and Raisin Sandwich	129

Creams
- Almond Crème Fraîche 31
- Applesauce Cream 23
- Cashew Cream for Granola 23
- Savory Cashew Cream 115
- Sour Cream 179
- Tofu Crème Fraîche 31
- Whipped Cream 49

Curried Cabbage	77
Curried Vegetables	181

D

Deli Slices	179
Dinner Roast Pot Pie	111

Dressings and Marinades
- Easy Salad Dressing or Marinade ... 87

Poppyseed Dressing for Fruit Salad 88
Raspberry Dressing 87
Sunny Isles Salad Dressing 88
Tofu and Dill Weed Dressing 86
Zesty Caribbean-Italian Dressing 88

E
Easy Guacamole 141
Eggplant Bake 99

F
Fried Cassava/White Yam 182
Fried Dumplings (Floats) 1 37
Fried Dumplings (Floats) 2 37
Frittata 38
Frosting 155
Fruited Yogurt Supreme 39

G
Game Night Sandwich 130
Garlic Bread 169
Glazed Baby Carrots 78
Gram Frittata 27
Granola
    Amazing Gluten-Free Granola 22
    Patty's Granola 21
    Simple Granola 22
Green Banana/Plantain Balls in Peanut Stew 178
Green Banana/Plantain with Stuffing 107
Grilled Pineapple 156
Grilled/Roasted Ripe Plantains 180

H
Hot Bean Sandwich 132

Hot Carob Tea 49
Hot Peppermint Chocolate Drink 49

J

Jamaican Ackee and "Tuna" 36
Jamaican Peanut Porridge 41
Jamaican Rice and Peas 113
Jeremy's Company Roast 105
Jerked Tofu 173
Juicy Fruit Salad 182

L

Lentils and Bulgur 113

M

Meatless Roast 105
Milks
    Almond Coconut Blend Milk 45
    Cashew-Sesame Milk 46
    Homemade Coconut Milk 174
    Organic Soybean Milk 46
    Vegan Condensed Milk 45
Mimi's Vegan Baked Macaroni Casserole 114
Mini Cheese Pizzas 172
Mock Chicken/Turkey Sandwich 133
Mock Chicken Salad 131
Mock Fish 108
Mock Omelet 20
Mock Tuna Salad 129
Mushroom Roast 101
Mushroom Sandwich 131
Mushroom and Soya Chunks Burgers 90
Mushroom and Water Chestnut Sauté 78

N
Nut Meat Balls 100

O
Oatmeal Meatballs 96
Onion Tofu Loaf 97
Overnight Prepared Buckwheat Groats 25

P
Pakasah 180
Parmesan Cheeze 169
Pancakes
    Easy Pancakes 29
    Fluffy Banana Pancakes 29
Party Wrap 134
PB, Carrots, and Raisin Sandwich 136
Pecan Meatballs 104
Peppered Gluten Strips 91
Pie Crust
    Basic Flaky Jamaican Pastry Crust 160
    Cookie Crust for Pies 160
    Pastry Crust 160
Pie in a Ramekin 92
Pita Pocket Sandwiches 133
Potatoes
    Hash Browns 170
    Oven Potatoes 33
    Potato Casserole 115
    Potatoes and Apples 77
    Potatoes with Tomato Sauce 91
    Sweet Potato Sticks 170

Q
Quiche 102

R

Rainbow Haystacks 95
Rainy Day Pakasa 106
Redi-burger® Red Top Roast 103
Rice Krispies® Loaf 108
Ripe Plantain Sandwich 136

S

Salads
- B.A.T. (Beans, Avocados, Tomatoes) Salad 82
- Beet and Carrot Salad 81
- Celery Salad 83
- Garbanzo Bean Salad 81
- Green Banana Salad 85
- Layered Potluck Salad 85
- Mango Salsa 84
- Salad in a Bag 83
- Sweet Potato Salad 84
- Waldorf Salad 82

Sauces
- Alfredo Sauce 120
- Basic Tomato Peanut Butter Sauce 126
- Basil Pesto 1 143
- Basil Pesto 2 144
- BBQ Sauce 118
- Black Pesto 144
- Dipping Sauce and Dressing 125
- Garlic Herb Sauce 119
- Ginger Sauce 123
- Lemon Cashew Sauce 122
- Meatballs and Sauce 124
- Peanut and Tomato Sauce 126
- Pesto Sauce for Root Vegetables 145
- Raspberry Sauce 118

Spinach Alfredo Sauce ... 120
  Sweet and Sour Sauce 1 ... 121
  Sweet and Sour Sauce 2 ... 121
  Tomato Sauce ... 123
  Tomatoes and Peanut Sauce ... 122
  Walnut Pesto ... 145
  White Sauce ... 124
  Whole Cranberry Sauce ... 119
Scones ... 159
Simple Sandwich ... 133
Smoothies and Slushes
  Bright Eyes Smoothie ... 54
  Creamy Mango Smoothie ... 44
  Easy Smoothie ... 50
  Gentle Greens Smoothie ... 54
  Immune Booster Smoothie ... 51
  Kids' Good Morning Smoothie ... 50
  Mango Ginger Lassie ... 48
  Melon and Ginger Cooler ... 54
  Morning Goodness Smoothie ... 50
  Party Punch ... 55
  Peachy Berry Smoothie ... 52
  Peanut Butter Punch ... 43
  Piña Colada ... 45
  Plantain Punch ... 55
  Roma® and Banana Latte ... 47
  Sparkling Mango Drink ... 43
  Strawberry Banana Nog ... 44
  Strawberry Slush ... 48
  Super Green Smoothie ... 53
  Tofu Pero® Latte ... 57
  Tropical Smoothie ... 51
Socca ... 40

Soft Rolls 161
Soppy's Trinidad Coconut Bake 34
Soups
    15-Bean Soup 66
    Black and Red Bean Soup 69
    Cream of Tomato Soup 70
    Cream Sauce for Cream Soup 70
    Crockpot Green Split Pea Soup 68
    Jamaican Red Bean Soup 67
    Lentil Soup 65
    Peanut Soup 1 62
    Peanut Soup 2 62
    Pumpkin and Bean Soup 63
    Pureed Pumpkin Soup 72
    Spinach Soup 64
    Vegetable Bounty Soup 64
Soy Yogurt 47
Special K® Roast 98
Spices and Seasonings
    Chicken-Style Seasoning 165
    Curry Mix 166
    Eden's Hope Seasoning Mix 164
    Fish-Style Seasoning 165
    Homemade Dry Spice 164
    Sesame Parmesan Seasoning 164
Spicy Sausage 34
Spreads
    Avocado Spread 140
    Blueberry Chia Spread 140
    Garbanzo Spread 139
    Not-Ham Sandwich Spread 140
    Party Spread 139
    Red Pepper Pâté 143

Sunflower and Sesame Seed Spread 146
Three Bean Spread 146
Steamed Callaloo 178
Stewed Gluten 102
Stews
   Black Bean Stew 72
   Gluten and Pigeon Peas Stew 74
   Okra Stew 74
   Plantain Balls for Stew or Soup 71
   Soy Curls with Lentils Stew 73
   Spinners for Soups and Stews 73
Strawberry Mold 157
Submarine Sandwich Filling 135

T

Tamale 93
Tofu Cutlets 107
Tofu Jerky 173
Tofu Ricotta 180
Tofu Rung Dung (Jamaican Style) 175
Tofu Spinach Triangles 172
Tofu Vegan Mayo 142
Tortilla Pot Pie 110
Tunol 35
Turned Corn Meal 171
TVP Curry 95

V

Vegetable Bacon 28
Vegetable Quesadillas 26
Vegetarian Baked Beans 99
Vegetarian Fritters 32

W
Waffles
- Hearty Waffles 27
- Potato Waffles 26

Y
Yellow Box Cake Surprise 158

About the Authors

Dorrel R. McLaren is a certified vegetarian food instructor, a well-seasoned chef, a trained lifestyle wellness and holistic life coach, a certified medical missionary, a personal fitness trainer, and nutrition specialist. She also earned a certificate in hospitality and tourism management and degrees in nutrition and organizational management.

She is married to Earl McLaren, a registered pharmacist. They have two adult children, Derrol and Samois; five grandchildren, Darielle, Christian, Gabrielle, Ayanna, and Daniel; and one great-granddaughter, LaNiyah.

Dorrel is very passionate about health and fitness and uses every opportunity to share and educate others. Her hobbies include developing new recipes, singing, laughing, spending time with loved ones over a healthy meal, traveling on mission trips, and observing people and their behavior. She has traveled around the United States, the Caribbean, and Africa, sharing the love of God by conducting exercise and cooking classes.

Her desire is to see each person fall in love with Jesus, serve Him always, develop healthy lifestyle habits, live life well and on purpose, and always treat people with respect.

Dorrel's motto is "Eat with the right attitude" and one of her favorite Bible texts is, "A bowl of vegetables with someone you love is better than steak with someone you hate" (Prov. 15:17, NLT).

***

Earl McLaren is a pharmacist with over thirty-five years of experience. He received his pharmaceutical training from the University of Technology School of Pharmacy (formerly C.A.S.T) in Jamaica, and from the University of Maryland School of Pharmacy in Baltimore, Maryland.

Earl also studied Nursing at Montgomery College, in Silver Spring, Maryland. He began his career as a unit dose and I.V. pharmacist at Suburban Hospital in

Bethesda, Maryland, and later worked as a retail pharmacist at the major chain stores of Giant, CVS, Rite Aid, and Target.

He also worked as a part-time specialty and compounding pharmacist at Theracom/CVS Procare Specialty pharmacy in Bethesda, Maryland, and later worked as pharmacy manager for three independent pharmacies. He is currently pharmacist-in-charge at Wye Oak Pharmacy in Baltimore, Maryland.

Earl and his wife Dorrel are co-founders of Eden's Hope Ministries. His role in this ministry includes lecturing and educating the public on pharmaceutical-related topics.

However, what he enjoys most is comedy, telling children's stories, and working with children. He was the children's choir director at Metropolitan SDA church for over thirty-five years. He is also director of Sounds of Culture and The EM group—both folk performing choral groups located in Maryland, and over the years, he has served as master of ceremonies for numerous weddings, anniversaries, birthday parties, and other special occasions. He also loves gardening and enjoys playing the guitar—a skill he taught one of his granddaughters. He is teaching his grandson how to play the bass guitar and his younger granddaughter how to play the piano.

He currently writes and presents devotionals snippets Thursday nights on the Forum at GCE (Globally Commissioned Evangelists), a telecommunicative prayer, evangelistic, and support ministry.

He has included a few of these devotionals in this cookbook with the hope of providing some spiritual appetizers ("spiritizers") to complement your physical nutrition.

Bon appetite!

TEACH Services, Inc.
P U B L I S H I N G

We invite you to view the complete
selection of titles we publish at:
www.TEACHServices.com

We encourage you to write us
with your thoughts about this,
or any other book we publish at:
info@TEACHServices.com

TEACH Services' titles may be purchased in
bulk quantities for educational, fund-raising,
business, or promotional use.
bulksales@TEACHServices.com

Finally, if you are interested in seeing
your own book in print, please contact us at:
publishing@TEACHServices.com

We are happy to review your manuscript at no charge.

www.ingramcontent.com/pod-product-compliance
Lightning Source LLC
Chambersburg PA
CBHW070942230426
43666CB00011B/2537